No Hot Water Tonight

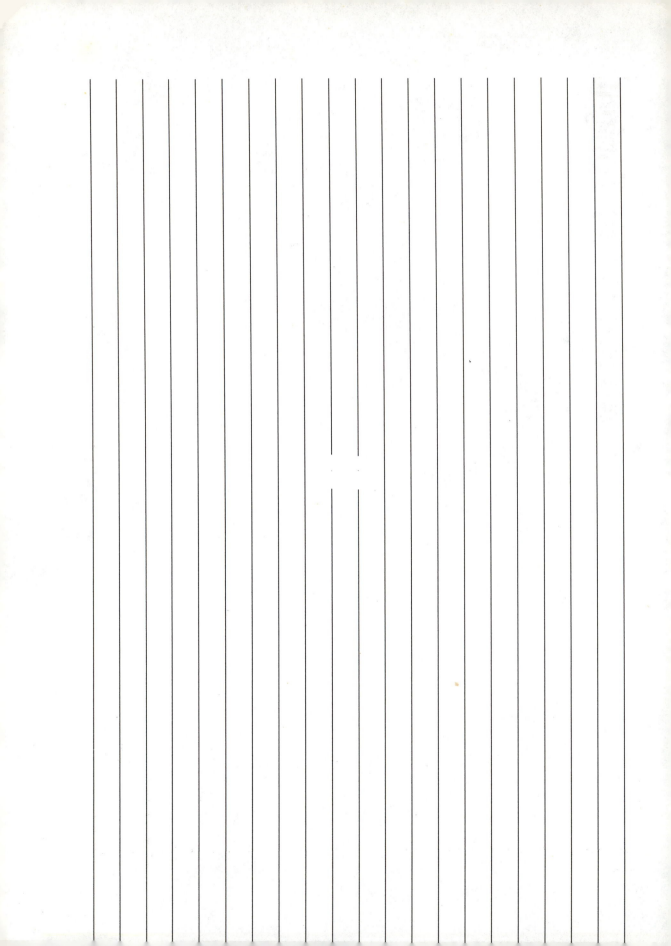

No Hot Water Tonight

Jean Bodman
Michael Lanzano

SECOND EDITION

MACMILLAN PUBLISHING COMPANY
New York

COLLIER MACMILLAN PUBLISHERS
London

Copyright © 1986, Macmillan Publishing Company, a division of Macmillan, Inc.

Printed in the United States of America

All rights reserved. No part of this book may be reproduced or transmitted in any form or by any means, electronic or mechanical, including photocopying, recording, or any information storage and retrieval system, without permission in writing from the publisher.

Earlier edition copyright © 1975 by Collier Macmillan International.

MACMILLAN PUBLISHING COMPANY
866 Third Avenue, New York, New York 10022

Collier Macmillan Canada, Inc.

Library of Congress Cataloging in Publication Data

Bodman, Jean.
    No hot water tonight.

    1. English language—Text-books for foreign speakers.
I. Lanzano, Michael.   II. Title
PE1128.B596   1986   428.2'4   85-8995
ISBN 0-02-311600-5

Printing: 1 2 3 4 5 6 7 8   Year: 6 7 8 9 0 1 2 3 4 5

ISBN   0-02-311600-5

Preface

We began writing *No Hot Water Tonight* in answer to the need for carefully controlled elementary readings that were adult in content and yet simple in structure. We have written a book that controls structure while being more liberal than most ESL texts with the introduction of vocabulary. Words that are necessary for survival in cities have been used whether they appear on work lists or not. The structural progression is similar to that used in most ESL beginning courses. Therefore, this reader can be used along with structural and functional textbooks in a complementary manner. But, most importantly, it can be used from the first weeks of class.

No Hot Water Tonight contains 25 chapters. Each chapter contains a reading selection followed by learning activities and comprehension exercises. The readings are all related to life in and around a tenement building in a city. Most of the incidents concern aspects of city life that adults must deal with: finding an apartment, dealing with the landlord, buying clothes and furniture, finding appropriate medical care, and so on.

In *No Hot Water Tonight*, we attempt to be as realistic as possible in our treatment of urban problems without being unduly pessimistic. Most, if not all, ESL texts portray American society as faultless. You do not find anxiety, loneliness, alienation, disease, or fear in ESL books, but these are precisely the emotions with which most newcomers can most easily identify. *No Hot Water Tonight* follows four or five sets of characters who live in the same tenement on 88th Street. The characters through whom the problems are explored and solved, or not solved, represent a cross section of an ethnically mixed, working class, and lower middle class neighborhood.

Our book is urban oriented and is especially designed for vocational programs, although it has been used successfully in academic ones. The content of the book was written to appeal to adolescents as well as adults.

J. B.
M. L.

Overview

The exercises in each chapter of *No Hot Water Tonight* are designed to appeal to several levels of students. It has been our experience that few ESL classes are homogeneously grouped (i.e., screened and pretested so that the class contains only those students with the same language abilities). Those few classes that *are* homogeneously grouped for oral work are rarely regrouped for reading. Therefore, the teacher has to accommodate students in the class who can read well and are capable of handling inferential questions for discussion, as well as those students who can only answer direct comprehension questions. In addition, we often find that students are assigned to our classes who have the ability to express themselves (however inaccurately) quite well, while others are severely limited in their ability to discourse in English. Therefore, we have designed exercises in each chapter to accommodate these students of differing abilities.

We recommend that *only* in Chapter 1 should teachers assign all the exercises. This will enable the teacher to note those students who complete the exercises easily and correctly. They can then be grouped together to do only more complex and/or advanced exercises. The students who work more slowly or who have errors on the simpler material can also be grouped together and assigned only the more basic exercises. If this book is used for intermediate level students, or if the teacher has several students of intermediate ability in the beginning reading class, the students can be encouraged to skip *all* the exercises in the first seven chapters and to use the initial chapters as extensive rather than intensive reading. After the seventh chapter, selected exercises may be assigned.

Therefore, this book has been written with the following premise in mind: The teacher of a particular class is best qualified to know the abilities of his or her students. The teacher should be free to pick and choose the exercises that will be most helpful and challenging for the students and skip over the others.

In each chapter a prereading section and a vocabulary list appear before the reading selection. The reading selection is then followed by cultural facts, comprehension exercises, vocabulary exercises, coping skill exercises, and, in several chapters, exercises designed to relate the story to the reader in a personalized way. Some chapters also contain supplementary readings.

The Prereading Section

Research has shown that reading comprehension can be greatly improved if students are thoughtfully prepared to read. Activities that stimulate the students' prior knowledge and experience as well as activities that give students experience with the vocabulary and structures to be encountered in the reading selection will raise the students' reading power. For this reason, three activities precede the reading selections: **Before You Read, Say These Words,** and **As You Read.**

Before You Read

The teacher may begin the class with a whole-group activity by asking the students to answer the questions in this section. However, we prefer to use small groups within the classroom. Therefore, although the teacher can ask the students these questions, we prefer that this task be assigned to a student in each group.

Say These Words

This section lists new vocabulary—words and phrases—that will appear in the reading selection. These words are grouped by common stress features. Words of one syllable appear first; words of two syllables with primary stress on the first syllable come next; followed by two-syllable words accented on the last syllable. Three- and four-syllable words follow. Teachers might wonder why we emphasize the pronunciation of these words when reading is primarily a silent activity. Research has shown that when readers are challenged by selections and find it necessary to read slowly, they will naturally begin to subvocalize in order to carry the meaning of the sentences more easily in their short-term memories. Because subvocalization is natural and helpful and because it is regularly employed by beginning ESL students, we have chosen to help the students pronounce more accurately the words they will encounter. If this section is to be taken up as a whole-group activity, the teacher can model the pronunciation and ask the students to repeat. The teacher should not turn this into a full-fledged pronunciation lesson but rather should merely take a minute or two to help the students become familiar with the sounds of the words.

The pronunciation of the words is only the first step in helping the students to become familiar with them. Establishing meaning for the new words is the second step. Our choice is to give the students some time to look over the word list. Then we ask them if there are any words that they do not know.

The following five techniques have proven helpful in aiding students to learn and retain new vocabulary.

1. Teachers can use pictures, objects, and mime where appropriate to establish meaning. For example, the word *building* can be illustrated by showing several pictures of different buildings.

2. Once meaning has been established, the teacher can try to make new words more memorable by using them in interesting contexts. For example, "Prince Charles is Diana's *husband*."

3. The teacher can relate new vocabulary to information gained in class about the students' personal lives. For example: "Haydee's apartment building is old. The elevator is no good. The paint is dirty in her apartment. Her building is *run down*. Everything is old. It's very *run down*."

4. Words are more likely to be retained if the students hear them used in a number of contexts that they generate themselves. That is to say, it is not enough for the teacher to use the words; the *students* must do so. For example, if the teacher wishes to teach the verb phrases "be sorry for" or "feel sorry for," the following strategy can be used. The teacher writes the verb phrases on the board. The teacher shows the students a picture of a man begging for money. The teacher can ask, "Do you *feel sorry for* him? Some people say yes. Some people say no. How do you feel?" Other pictures from the newspaper or current magazines can be used to give more practice.

5. Perhaps the best strategy for teaching words, if your students will cooperate, is to ask them to read the selection first to see if they can discover the meanings of the words from the context. We tell the students, "Read it first. Then, if you don't understand the story, go back and find the words that are giving you trouble. Look up these words in a bilingual dictionary, ask a classmate to help you with them, or ask the teacher." Needless to say, experienced ESL teachers know that some students will ask the teacher, while others will insist on immediate translation via a dictionary or a classmate. Faced with firmly entrenched learning habits, our advice is, surrender! Let the students use their own learning strategies. If some students want to look up all the words, so be it. Encourage them to read the whole story first, then go back. If they do not follow this advice and prefer to amass long lists of words in their notebooks, they will soon find that as the stories get longer and the vocabulary "load" increases, the teacher's strategy is better.

As a teacher you should not worry if the new vocabulary items are not all learned or retained. Do your best to make the words meaningful, and try to show the students that the new words are useful. You will not be able to force learning to take place. Learning will occur in its own time and at its own pace. If the students in your class live in the inner city, they often will encounter the words used in this book. The words that *need* to be learned *will* be learned.

One final word on vocabulary: Please don't let yourself be tempted to teach those words that the students already know just because the words appear on a list at the beginning of each chapter. If a student can use the word in the correct way in the correct context, resist the temptation of dragging out those lovely pictures you spent half the night gathering, and go immediately to the next item. Most of the time in the class should be spent reading and discussing—not learning interminable lists of vocabulary words.

As You Read

The purpose of this section is to help the student to anticipate the main events or the important information in the reading selection. Just reading over these questions will help the students to understand the selection better and to increase their reading speed.

The Reading Section

In presenting the reading selection we have varied our methods, all of which have worked well. Here are some guidelines.

Students should always be given a chance to read the selection silently to themselves before any other activities take place. Thereafter, the teacher may do the following:

1. Read the selections out loud with natural intonation.
2. Have the students take the various roles in the book.
3. Tape the selections and have American friends play the roles of the characters in the book.
4. Have the students go directly to the comprehension exercises.

Cultural Facts

Items of interest to students from different cultures are presented here to help them better understand the reading selection. In the beginning chapters, where we anticipate that the students' command of English is very limited, there are no discussion questions. In later chapters, we invite the students to compare statements made about life in this country to that in their native lands.

The Comprehension Exercises

As suggested in the beginning of the Overview, we strongly recommend that the students be given selective exercises according to their abilities. Do not spend too much time on any one item unless the students show great interest in continuing the discussion.

The Vocabulary Exercises

If possible, assign these exercises for homework. Vocabulary, to be learned, often needs time for repetition and contemplation.

The Supplementary Readings

The teacher should let the students read these selections by themselves and resist the temptation to teach this section. This reading is just for pleasure.

Supplementary Grammar Exercises

Some supplementary grammar exercises are included at the end of the book. They are intended not to give practice in every structure in the book but rather to reinforce work that may have already taken place in the grammar portion of the class or to give students practice with new structures needed to comprehend the reading selections.

If the teacher does not feel that the students need this added practice, then the exercises do not have to be assigned.

The Content of the Book

As stated previously, we have included topics in this book not usually found in ESL texts. Some teachers feel that they must direct part of the discussion period of the lesson to present a more "balanced" view of American life. We feel that this is an excellent idea as long as the teacher does not turn the discussion into a lecture. The young boy in the story has problems in his relationship with his mother. Some teachers feel it necessary to tell their students that not all American children are this way. Our suggestion, however, is to elicit this statement from the students themselves by asking questions: "Is Bobby a typical American boy? Are all American boys like Bobby? Are some boys in your country like Bobby?" and so forth.

Other topics that teachers may want to deal with are: the position of women in society in reference to Barbara and her naiveté; the impersonality of bureaucratic institutions in relation to Bobby and Mrs. Gold's experience at the hospital; the concept of the family and the neighborhood, which are referred to throughout the book; and the implications of immigration. The teacher should remember that nonnative speaking students often tend to be politically and socially (in terms of social change, i.e., the women's movement) more conservative. This book has been designed to provoke discussion on many of these topics; however, some classes will not care to deal with philosophical problems when they have so many day-to-day survival problems. Let the students be the guide in the classroom, and do not force them to assume American liberal or conservative attitudes. For example, we thought that we had presented Barbara as a scatter-brained, subservient wife. What a surprise when we asked a particular class their opinion of her. They thought that she was very up-to-date and liberated. We asked the students to identify how she was up-to-date. The response was fascinating—she bought her own clothes without her husband having to accompany her!

In conclusion, we have written the book to appeal to as many levels and as many types of students as possible. The exercises are designed so that students may interact with one another independently of the teacher. We feel that the value of the readings will be lessened if the teacher inadvertently incurs student boredom from excessive class time on exercises. We hope that the chapters will be covered rapidly in class and that the students will be encouraged to read on by themselves if they do not need supervision—after all, there is always *No Cold Water, Either!*

Contents

No Hot Water Tonight

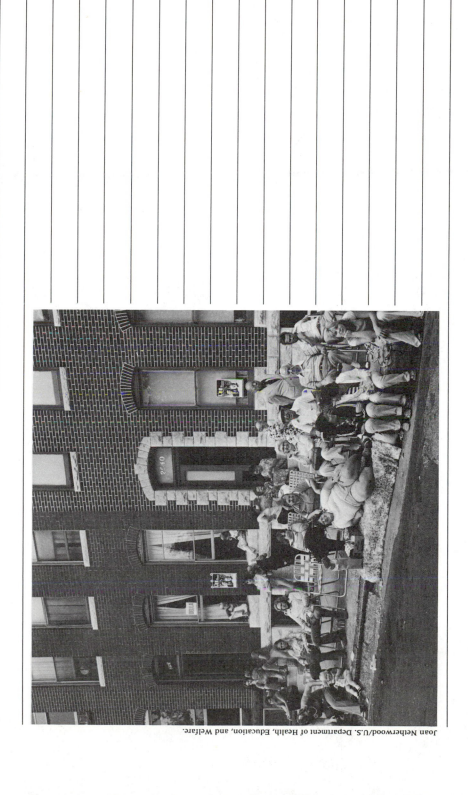

Joan Netherwood/U.S. Department of Health, Education, and Welfare.

Before you read, answer these questions:

What's your name?
Where are you from?
Are you married or single?
Where's your apartment, room, or house?

Say these words after your teacher or after an American friend:

name	daugh' ter	
dead	build' ing	
son	Eur' ope	
still	mar' ried	
young	sin' gle	
old	neigh' bor	
life	cit' y	

Phrases
the same
Latin America

hel' lo   a lone'
win' dow   dif' fer ent
morn' ing   af ter noon'
hus' band   in' ter est ing
eve' ning

As you read, think about these questions:

Who is Mrs. Gold?
Where is she?
Why is she alone?
Who are her neighbors?
Why are they interesting?

This is a story about Mrs. Gold. Her apartment is in this building.

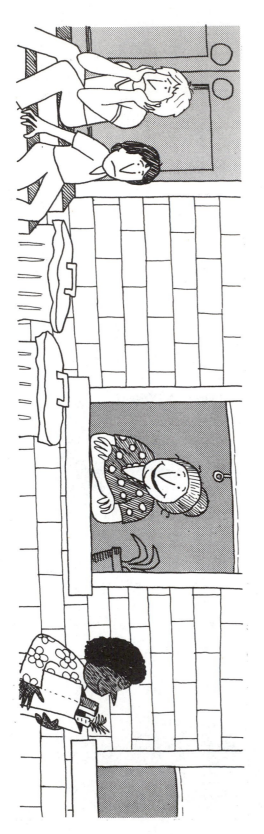

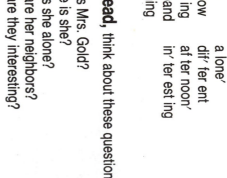

MRS. GOLD

Hello. My name is Mrs. Gold. Here I am every day—here at my window. In the morning, in the afternoon, and in the evening I am here—alone. My husband is dead, and my son and daughter are married. I am still here in the same city, in the same building.

The people in this building are interesting. They are different. Some are from Europe. Some are from Latin America. Some are married, and some are single. Married, single, young, or old, we are neighbors. Their life is my life now.

Cultural facts

Times of the Day in the United States

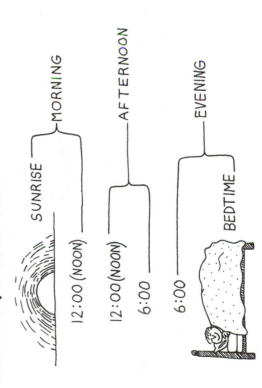

Is it the same in your country?

COMPREHENSION EXERCISES

Finding the Facts

If the sentence is true, write "T." If the sentence is false, write "F."

For example:

<u>T</u> Mrs. Gold says she is at her window every day.
<u>F</u> Her daughter is single.

1. ＿＿ Mrs. Gold's husband is dead.

2. ＿＿ Her daughter is married.

3. ＿＿ Her son is married.

4. ＿＿ Some people in the building are single.

5. ＿＿ Some people in the building are from Europe.

Making Inferences

If, in your opinion, the sentence is true, write "T." If, in your opinion, the sentence is false, write "F."

1. ＿＿ Mrs. Gold is an old lady.

2. ＿＿ Mrs. Gold is happy with her life.

3. ＿＿ People from different countries are interesting to Mrs. Gold.

4. ＿＿ Her neighbors are like her family.

Stating Facts

1. Tell me about Mrs. Gold.

a. _She's at the window everyday._

b. _____

c. _____

d. _____

2. Tell me about her neighbors.

a. _____

b. _____

c. _____

d. _____

3. Write the answers to the following questions:

Example:

Is Mrs. Gold's husband alive or dead?

He's dead.

a. Are her children married or single?

_____

b. Is her building new or old?

_____

c. Is she at her window or at her door every day?

_____

d. Is she usually alone or not?

_____

e. Are people in her building from different countries or not?

_____

Exercise for More Advanced Students: Stating Opinions

Write or discuss the answers to the following questions:

1. Why is Mrs. Gold alone?
2. Why is Mrs. Gold in the same building after so many years?
3. Why is Mrs. Gold at her window all the time?

VOCABULARY EXERCISE

Look at these words:

√ *building*   *afternoon*
window   *evening*
morning

Wr'te the correct word in the sentences that follow.

1. What's this?
   It's a *building* .

1

2. What time of day is it?
   It's _____ .

2

3. What's this?
   It's a _____ .

3

4. What time of day is it?
   It's _____ .

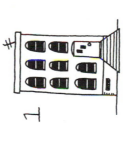

4

5. He's in school. What time of day is it?
   It's _____ .

5

MY STORY

This is your story. Write the correct information in the empty spaces. Tell me about yourself.

Hello. My name is _____. Here I am—here
                       (your name)

_____. The students in my class are interesting.
(where are you now?)

They are different. Some are from _____. Some are
                              (a country or a city)

from _____. Some are _____, and
   (a different country or city)   *(young, old, married?)*

some are _____. We are classmates.
       (young, etc.)

For *Grammar Practice*, see page 180.

2

U.S. Department of Housing and Urban Development.

Before you read, answer these questions:

Where's your husband, wife, daughter, son, mother, father, or best friend?

Is that person very busy now?

How old are you?

How old are your friends?

Say these words after your teacher or after an American friend:

		Phrases
sure	bus' y	be at home
boy	on' ly	be at home
friend	la' dy	be at work
ne' ver	o kay'	

As you read, think about these questions:

Where's Bobby's mother?

How old are Bobby's friends?

How old is Bobby?

Is Bobby angry at Mrs. Gold?

This chapter is a conversation between Mrs. Gold and a young boy. His name is Bobby.

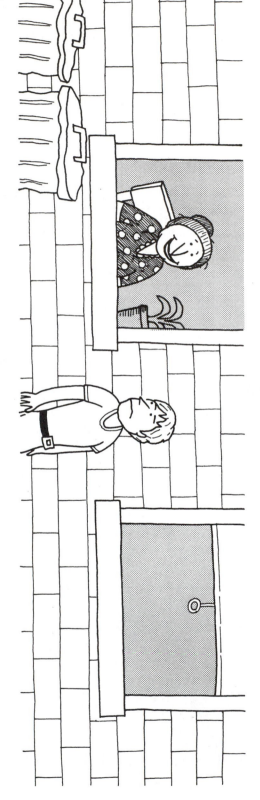

YOU'RE AN OLD LADY

Mrs. Gold: Bobby! Hello, Bobby!

Bobby: What?

Mrs. Gold: How are you, Bobby?

Bobby: Okay.

Mrs. Gold: Where's your mother? Is she at home?

Bobby: No. She's at work. She's never home.

Mrs. Gold: I'm sure she's very busy.
Bobby: Sure. Sure.
Mrs. Gold: Who are those boys?
Bobby: They're my friends. Why?
Mrs. Gold: How old are they?
Bobby: Eighteen or nineteen. Why?
Mrs. Gold: But Bobby, you're only fourteen.
Bobby: Yes, and you're an old lady.
Mrs. Gold: Bobby!

Cultural facts

Working Mothers in the United States

Bobby's mother is at work today. Most American women work these days. Look at this information:

Mothers Who Work (figures in percentages)

Year	Their children are 1 month to 6 years old	Their children are 6 years to 17 years old
1950	13.6%	32.8%
1955	18.2%	38.4%
1965	25.5%	45.7%
1975	38.9%	54.8%
1976	39.7%	56.2%
1977	40.9%	58.3%
1978	43.7%	60.0%
1979	45.4%	61.6%

Is it the same in your country?

COMPREHENSION EXERCISES

Finding the Facts

If the sentence is true, write "T." If the sentence is false, write "F."

1. _____ Bobby says he is not okay.

2. _____ Bobby is 18 years old.

3. _____ Bobby's friends are 14 years old.

4. _____ Bobby says his mother is not at work.

5. _____ Bobby says Mrs. Gold is an old lady.

Making Inferences

If, in your opinion, the sentence is true, write "T." If, in your opinion, the sentence is false, write "F."

1. _____ Bobby is not happy about Mrs. Gold's questions.

2. _____ Bobby's mother is never at home.

3. _____ Mrs. Gold is not happy about Bobby's friends.

4. _____ Mrs. Gold is an old lady.

5. _____ Bobby is nice to Mrs. Gold.

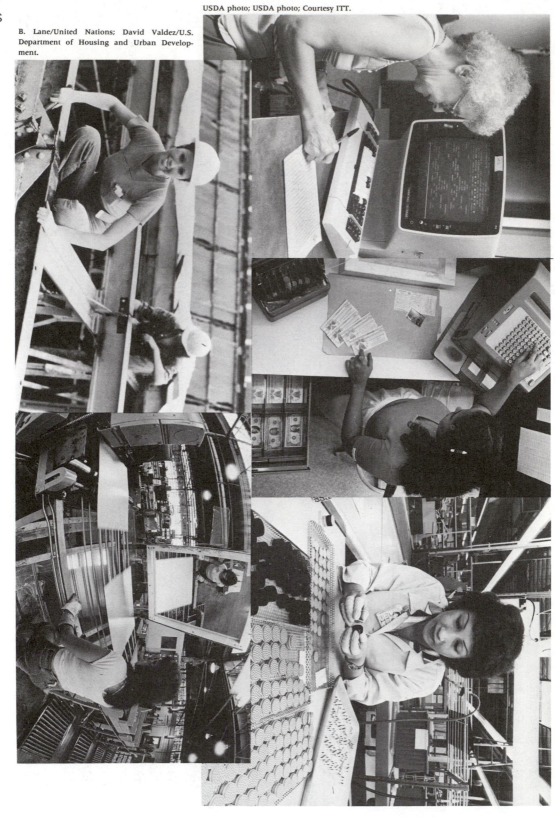

Stating Facts

1. Tell me four things about Bobby.

   a. _____

   b. _____

   c. _____

   d. _____

2. Tell me two things about Bobby's mother.

   a. _____

   b. _____

3. Tell me two things about Bobby's friends.

   a. _____

   b. _____

4. Write the answers to the following questions:

   a. Is Bobby's mother home or at work?

   _____

   b. Are Bobby's friends 14 years old or 18 and 19 years old?

   _____

Exercise for More Advanced Students: Stating Opinions

Write or discuss the answers to the following questions:

1. Bobby says his mother is never home. Do you think this is true?

2. Do you think Bobby loves his mother? Why or why not?

3. Why does Bobby say, "Yes, and you're an old lady?"

4. Is Mrs. Gold surprised or angry when Bobby says, "Yes, and you're an old lady"?

FREE READING

New Vocabulary

yeah	wo´ man
wow	al´ ways
hey	fun´ ny
kid	to day´
girl	**Phrases and expressions**
late	What's happening?
no´ thing	Take it easy.
birth´ day	

You're a Funny Kid

Bobby: What's happening, Jim?

   Jim: Nothing, kid.

Bobby: Isn't your birthday today?

Jim: Yeah. I'm eighteen.

Bobby: Wow!

Jim: Yeah. How old are you, kid?

Bobby: Uh . . . sixteen.

Jim: Oh, yeah?

Bobby: Okay. I'm fifteen.

How's your girl?

Jim: Okay. What time is it, kid?

Bobby: About 7:30.

Jim: She's late.

Bobby: Women are always late.

Jim: Oh, yeah?

Bobby: Yeah.

Jim: You're a funny kid. There she is. Hey . . . Judy . . . over here. Take it easy, kid.

Bobby: Yeah. Take it easy.

For Grammar Practice, see page 180.

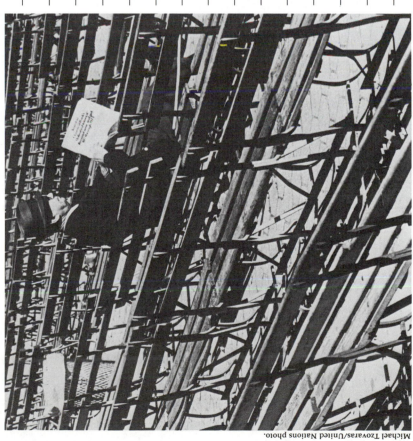

Michael Tzovaras/United Nations photo.

Before you read, answer these questions:

Are you happy today?
What are you happy about?
Are you worried about anything?
What are you worried about?

Say these words after your teacher or after an American friend:

too
all
new
just
an′ gry
prob′ lem
mo′ ther

us′ ual ly
neigh bor′ hood
re ac′ tion

Phrases

feel sorry for
be in school
be worried about
be right
be _____ business

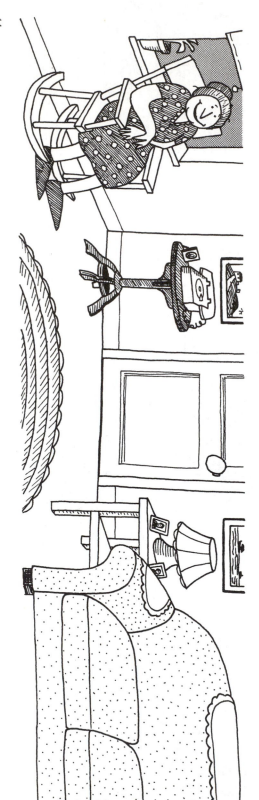

As you read, think about these questions:

Is Mrs. Gold angry at Bobby?
How does she feel about Bobby?
Who is Mrs. Curtis?
Why is Mrs. Gold worried about her?

Mrs. Gold is at her window, as usual. There is no one around. The street is quiet. She's worried.

MRS. GOLD'S REACTION

(*thinking to herself*) That's Bobby Curtis. Angry? No, I'm not angry. Bobby's a problem. I feel sorry for him. And his mother—I feel sorry for her, too. She's at work all day. Bobby's usually in school, but today he's with those boys. Who are those boys? They're new in the neighborhood. Where are they from? I'm worried.

Yes, Bobby's right. It isn't any of my business. Bobby isn't my son. I'm just an old lady.

Where's Mrs. Curtis? What time is it? It's 5:30. She's usually home at 5:15. Where is she? Why is she late?

Cultural facts

The Work Day in the United States
Mrs. Curtis is a blue collar worker. She's at work from 8:00 to 5:00.

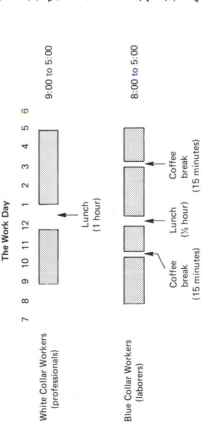

The Work Day

White Collar Workers (professionals) — 9:00 to 5:00
Lunch (1 hour)

Blue Collar Workers (laborers) — 8:00 to 5:00
Coffee break (15 minutes)
Lunch (½ hour)
Coffee break (15 minutes)

Is the work day the same in your country?

COMPREHENSION EXERCISES

Finding the Facts

If the sentence is true, write "T." If the sentence is false, write "F."

1. ___ Mrs. Gold is angry.

2. ___ Mrs. Gold feels sorry for Mrs. Curtis.

3. ___ Bobby is usually in school.

4. ___ Bobby's last name is Gold.

5. ___ Mrs. Curtis is usually home at 5:30.

Making Inferences

If, in your opinion, the sentence is true, write "T." If, in your opinion, the sentence is false, write "F."

1. ___ Mrs. Gold is worried about the new boys in the neighborhood.

2. ___ Bobby is not in school today.

3. ___ Mrs. Gold is worried about Mrs. Curtis.

4. ___ Bobby is new in the neighborhood.

5. ___ Mrs. Curtis is at home.

Stating Facts

1. Tell me something about Bobby's mother.

   a. _____

   b. _____

2. Tell me something new about Mrs. Gold.

   a. _____

   b. _____

   c. _____

3. Write the answers to the following questions:

Example:
Is Mrs. Gold worried about Bobby or angry at him?

She's worried about him.

   a. Is Bobby in school today or with his friends?

   b. Is Bobby's last name Curtis or Gold?

_____

_____

Exercise for More Advanced Students: Stating Opinions

Write or discuss the answers to the following questions:

1. Why isn't Bobby in school? (Give several possibilities.)

2. Why is Mrs. Gold worried?
3. Why does Mrs. Gold feel sorry for Bobby? (Give several possibilities.)

VOCABULARY EXERCISE

Answer the following exercise from memory. Read the original story again (p. 15). Then read the following story. Select the correct word. Then circle it.

That's Bobby Curtis. Angry? No, I'm not (*angry new late*). Bobby's a (*problem father lady*). I feel (*happy sorry*) for him. And his (*mother sister friend*)—I feel sorry for her, too. She's at (*school work home*) all day. Bobby's (*never not usually*) in school, but today he's with those (*children girls boys*). Who are those (*boys men girls*)? They're (*bad new rich*) in the (*window school neighborhood*). Where are they from? I'm (*worried angry*).

Yes, Bobby's right. It isn't any of my (*school business apartment*). Bobby isn't my (*grandson son father*). I'm just an old (*girl lady teacher*). Where's Mrs. Curtis? What (*minute day time*) is it? It's 5:30. She's usually home at (*6:00 5:15 10:00*). Where is she? Why is she (*here sorry late*)?

For *Grammar Practice*, see page 181.

4

U.S. Department of Housing and Urban Development.

Before you read, answer these questions:

Tell me about your apartment, room, or house.

Is it good or bad?

Is it large or small?

Is it in a city or not?

Are you ever afraid when you're in your home in the United States?

Are you ever afraid when you're in the street near your home? Why or why not?

Say these words after your teacher or after an American friend:

		Phrases and expressions
street	peo′ ple	thrift shop
block	ware′ house	in good condition
bad	lock′ smith	run down
store	ceil′ ing	dry cleaners
bar	emp′ ty	

wall	bou tique′	at night
floor	a fraid′	
stairs	a′ ve nue	
rent	rob′ bery	
crime	res′ tau rant	
ve′ ry	a part′ ment	
build′ ing	for′ tunetel ler	

As you read, think about these questions:

What's on 88th Street?

Are there any stores?

Is 88th Street between Second Avenue and Third Avenue a good block?

Why are the people worried?

This story is about 88th Street and the people on the street.

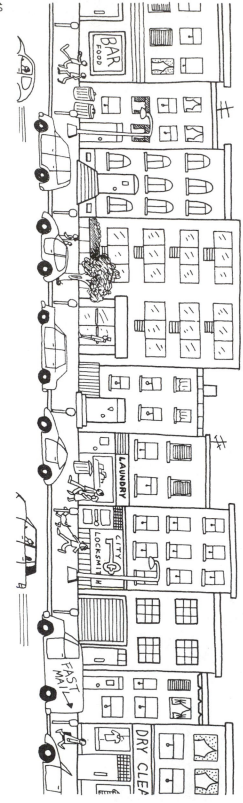

18

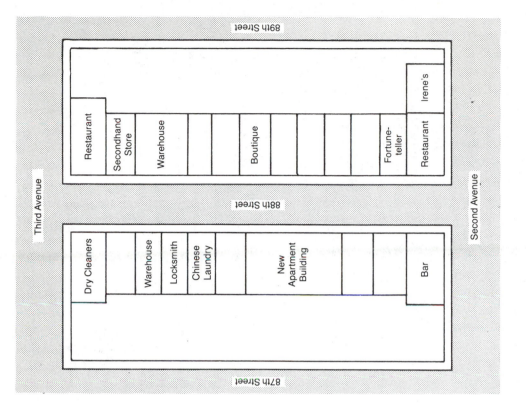

THE STREET

This is 88th Street between Second and Third Avenue. It isn't a very good block, but it isn't very bad.

There are a lot of apartment buildings here. Some are in good condition. Some old ones are very run down.

There are two restaurants, two warehouses, a dry cleaners, a thrift shop, a boutique, a locksmith, a bar, and a fortuneteller, too.

The people in the old apartment buildings are worried. Everything in their buildings is old: the walls, the floors, the ceilings, the stairs. Everything.

The people in the new buildings aren't worried about the condition of their buildings. They're worried about their rent.

The people are worried about the block. They are worried about crime. There are robberies every day. The street is empty at night because the people are afraid. That's 88th Street.

Cultural facts

Cities and Suburbs in the United States

In cities, the stores and the apartment buildings are on the same street.

In suburbs, the houses are sometimes a mile or two from the stores. Families need a car.

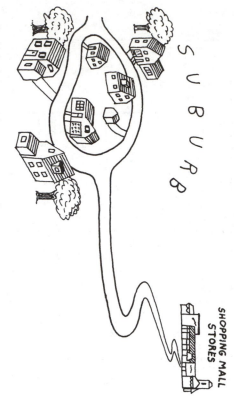

SUBURB

SHOPPING MALL STORES

Is it the same in your country?

COMPREHENSION EXERCISES

Finding the Facts

If the sentence is true, write "T." If the sentence is false, write "F."

1. —— There are a lot of apartment buildings on this block.

2. —— 88th Street between Second Avenue and Third Avenue isn't a very good block.

3. —— It isn't a very bad block.

4. —— There are a lot of grocery stores on this block.

5. —— There are restaurants and warehouses on this block.

6. —— Some buildings are run down.

7. —— The people are worried about the bar.

8. —— The people in the new apartment buildings are worried about their buildings.

9. —— There are robberies every day.

10. —— The street is empty at night because the people are happy.

11. —— The people are worried about crime.

12. —— This story is about 98th Street.

Exercise for More Advanced Students: Making Inferences

If, in your opinion, the sentence is true, write "T." If, in your opinion, the sentence is false, write "F."

1. —— The people on 88th Street are rich.

2. —— Some people are afraid of their buildings.

3. —— The new buildings are in bad condition.

4. —— The rents in the new buildings are high.

Stating Facts

1. Tell me about the buildings on 88th Street.

a. _____

b. _____

c. _____

2. Tell me about the people in the apartment buildings.

a. _____

b. _____

c. _____

VOCABULARY EXERCISES

Select one word for every empty space in the story. Write the correct word in the correct space. Use each word only one time.

Use these words in Paragraph One:
Avenue   bad
good   √ Street

Paragraph One

This is 88th _Street_ between Second Avenue and Third _____. It isn't a very _____ block. It isn't very _____.

Use these words in Paragraph Two:
run down   condition   apartment

Paragraph Two

There are a lot of _____ buildings here. Some are in good _____. Some old ones are very _____.

Use these words in Paragraph Three:
bar   two

Paragraph Three

There are two restaurants, _____ warehouses, a dry cleaners, a thrift shop, a boutique, a locksmith, a _____, and a fortuneteller, too.

Use these words in Paragraph Four:
ceilings   buildings

Paragraph Four

The people in the old apartment _____ are worried. Everything in their buildings is old: the walls, the floors, the ——————, the stairs, the kitchens, the bath-rooms. Everything.

Use these words in Paragraph Five:

rent   people   worried

Paragraph Five

The —————— in the new buildings aren't —————— about the condition of their buildings. They're worried about their ——————.

Use these words in Paragraph Six:

robberies   people
crime   night
worried

Paragraph Six

The people are —————— about the block. They are worried about ——————. There are —————— every day. The street is empty at —————— because the —————— are afraid. That's 88th Street.

A More Difficult Vocabulary Exercise

The following is an exercise for more advanced students. Look at the following words:

22

restaurant	locksmith
fortuneteller	bar
dry cleaners	boutique
thrift shop	
apartment	
building	

Select a word to fill each empty space that follows.

1. What kind of store is this?

It's a —————— .

PAR-NYC.

U.S. Department of Health, Education, and Welfare.

PAR-NYC.

3. What kind of store is this?

   Oh, that's easy. It's a ——————.

PAR-NYC.

2. What kind of store is this?

   That's a ——————.

4. What kind of place is this?

   It looks like a ——————.

24

PAR-NYC.

PAR-NYC.

5. What kind of place is this?

I know. That's a ―――――.

6. What kind of store is this?

It looks like a ―――――
―――――.

USDA photo.

PAR-NYC.

7. What kind of a building is this?

Oh, for sure, that's an ——————————.

8. What kind of place is this?

I'm not sure, but I think that's a ——————————.

MY NEIGHBORHOOD

This is your story. Write some information about yourself in the empty spaces.

    This is my neighborhood. My _____ is on
(apartment house room)

_____ between _____ and _____ .

There are a lot of _____ on my block. There

is also a _____ , a _____ , and a

_____ .

    The people on my block are happy about

_____ .

    Some people are worried about _____ .

Other people are worried about _____ .

The streets are _____ at night because

_____ .

For _Grammar Practice_, see page 182.

U.S. Department of Housing and Urban Development.

Before you read, answer these questions:

What time are you usually home by?
What time are you usually in bed by?
What are the names of your neighbors?
Are your neighbors your friends?

Say these words after your teacher or after an American friend:

bus	ti' red
run	eas' y
poor	rea' dy
man	may' be
wife	din' ner
dumb	good bye'
work	ter' ri ble
ear' ly	pro' ba bly

Phrases and expressions

Good evening.
Good night.
for once
on time
be glad (that)
Have a nice _____.

As you read, think about these questions:

Who is Mr. Torres?
Why is he home early today?
Why is he glad his daughters are home?
Is Mr. Torres Bobby's friend?

The next dialogue is between Mrs. Gold and Mr. Torres. They aren't friends, but they're neighbors.

MRS. GOLD AND MR. TORRES

Mrs. Gold: Good evening, Mr. Torres. Aren't you home early today?

Mr. Torres: What time is it?

Mrs. Gold: It's 5:30. You're usually home at 6:00.

Mr. Torres: Am I? The buses are running on time, for once.

Mrs. Gold: Those buses! It's terrible for you poor, tired men. You're tired, and they're late. Terrible.

Mr. Torres: Well, that's life.

Mrs. Gold: Terrible.

Mr. Torres: Is my wife home?

Mrs. Gold: Yes. She's home and your girls are, too.

Mr. Torres: Good. I'm glad the girls are home. My wife and I are worried about those new boys in the neighborhood.

Mrs. Gold: I am, too. Where are they from? I'm worried about Bobby.

Mr. Torres: Isn't he home?

Mrs. Gold: No, he's with those boys.

Mr. Torres: He is? Dumb kid. Where's his mother? Isn't she home?

Mrs. Gold: No. She's working.

Mr. Torres: Life isn't easy for working mothers.

Mrs. Gold: No. Life isn't easy. Mr. Torres? Maybe you and Bobby . . .

Mr. Torres: Well, dinner is probably ready. Good-bye, Mrs. Gold.

Mrs. Gold: Bobby and . . . Oh yes. Have a nice evening, Mr. Torres.

Mr. Torres: Good night.

Mrs. Gold: Yes. Yes. Maybe Bobby and Mr. Torres . . .

Cultural facts

Transportation in the United States

In the suburbs in the United States and in a few cities like Los Angeles, most people go to work in cars. In large cities, people go to work by bus or train. A small number of people take boats or ride motor-cycles or bicycles to work. Very few people walk.
Is it the same in your country?

Meal Times in the United States

Most families eat breakfast and dinner together. Most children eat lunch at school. Workers do not usually go home for lunch.

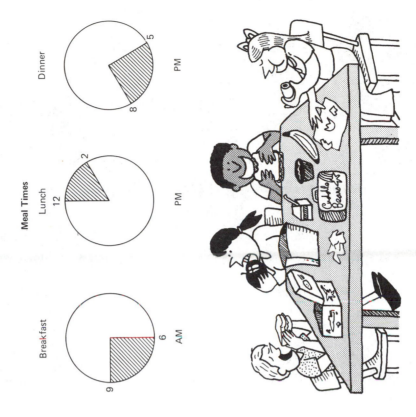

Meal Times

Breakfast — 9, 6 AM

Lunch — 12, 2 PM

Dinner — 8, 5 PM

Is it the same in your country?

COMPREHENSION EXERCISES

Finding the Facts

If the sentence is true, write "T." If the sentence is false, write "F."

1. _____ Mrs. Torres is at work.

2. _____ Bobby is home.

3. _____ The buses are on time all the time.

4. _____ It's 6:00.

5. _____ Mr. Torres is usually home at 5:30.

Making Inferences

If, in your opinion, the sentence is true, write "T." If, in your opinion, the sentence is false, write "F."

1. _____ Mr. Torres is Bobby's father.

2. _____ Mr. Torres is probably tired.

3. _____ Mr. Torres is very worried about Bobby.

4. _____ Mr. Torres is worried about the buses.

5. _____ Mr. Torres is poor.

Stating Facts

Tell me four things about Mr. Torres and his family.

1. _____

2. _____

3. _____

4. _____

Write the answers to the following questions:

1. Are the buses running on time or late today?
2. Is Mr. Torres home early or late today?
3. Is Mr. Torres' wife usually home before him or after him?
4. Is Mrs. Curtis at home or working?

Discussion Questions

Write or discuss the answers to the following questions:

1. What time is it now?
2. What time are you usually home by?
3. Are you ever late? Why?
4. Are you ever tired? When?

Finish this sentence in two different ways. Write or discuss your answers.

1. Sometimes I think life is _____

2. Sometimes I think life is _____

Finish this sentence in two different ways:

1. Life isn't easy for _____

2. Life isn't easy for _____

Discussion Questions for More Advanced Students

Finish the following sentences. Write or discuss your answers.

1. Life is easy when _____

2. People are happy when _____

3. I'm angry when _____

VOCABULARY EXERCISES

Select the correct word for each empty space in the sentences below. Use each word only once.

buses   √wife   early

My ___*wife*___ is home _____ today because the _____ are running on time.

on time   for a change

Usually the subways are late, but today they are _____ ' _____ .

life   working

My husband is a _____ man. _____ isn't easy for us.

dinner   tired   probably

Mr. Torres: Is _____ ready?

Daughter: _____ .

Mr. Torres: Good. I'm very _____ and hun-gry this evening.

Vocabulary from Context

Look at the story on p. 28. There are three ways to say *good-bye* after 5:00. One is *good-bye*. Write two other ways.

1. _good-bye_
2. _____
3. _____

For *Grammar Practice*, see page 183.

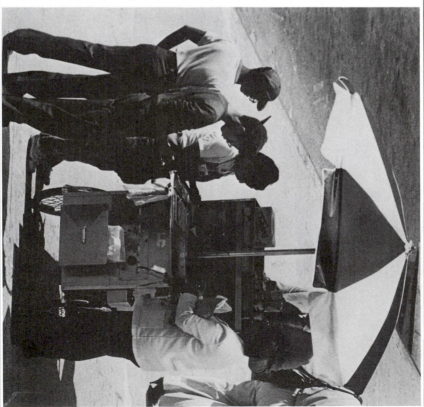

U.S. Department of Housing and Urban Development.

Before you read, answer these questions:

Is your apartment (room, house) quiet or noisy?
Is there a lot of noise on your street or is it quiet?
What kinds of sounds are there during the day?
What kinds of sounds are there during the night?
Think of your country. What sounds in your country are different
    from the sounds here?
Tell me about the music in your country.

Say these words after your teacher or after an American friend:

sound	bang	ball	chil′ dren	come in
voice	click	shout	op′ en	right away
give	come	ask	noi′ sy	
		call	si′ ren	
		right	ta′ ble	
		car	op′ er a	
		day	fi′ re	
		truck	mu′ sic	
		move	gar′ bage	
		rock	ma chine′	
		soup	po lice′	
		noise	clas′ si cal	
		horn	pop′ u lar	
		close (v.)	am′ bu lance	

Phrases and expressions

Come on
Your old lady

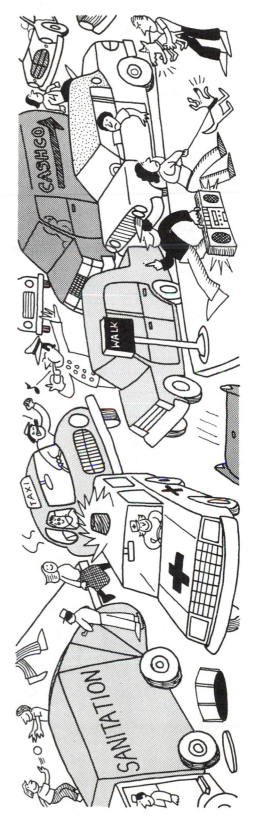

35

As you read, think about these questions:

What kinds of sounds are there in the city?
Are there good sounds?
Are there noises?
Why is Bobby's mother calling him?

This story is about life on 88th Street. It's a story about the sounds of life there.

THE SOUNDS OF THE STREET

Sounds. The sounds of life on 88th Street. There are the voices of children.

"Give me the ball!"

There are the shouts of boys.

"Come on. Ask your old lady for a dollar."

There are the calls of mothers.

"Bobby! Come in for dinner. Bobby? Right away. Now."

There are the sounds of cars. All day, all night, cars and trucks are moving down 88th Street. There is the sound of music from open windows: opera, classical, popular, rock. All at the same time—a music soup.

Noises. The city is noisy. There are the noises of horns, of ambulance sirens, police sirens, and fire sirens, of machines, and of garbage trucks. There are the noises of doors closing. Bang. Click.

"Bobby. This is the last time. Dinner's on the table."
"Okay. Okay. I'm coming."

"Now, Bobby."
"Okay. Yeah. Take it easy."

Cultural facts

Recorded Music in the United States

Many teenagers and some adults are always listening to music. Look around you. Walking on the street, running in the park, sitting on buses, trains, and planes; eating, playing, studying, and working, Americans are listening to music. What are they listening to?

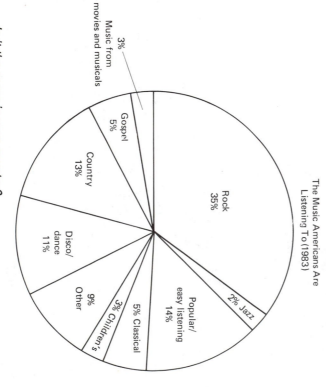

The Music Americans Are Listening To (1983)

Rock 35%

2% Jazz

Popular/ easy listening 14%

5% Classical

3% Children's

9% Other

Disco/ dance 11%

Country 13%

Gospel 5%

3% Music from movies and musicals

Is it the same in your country?

COMPREHENSION EXERCISES

Finding the Facts

If the sentence is true, write "T." If the sentence is false, write "F."

1. ____ The city isn't noisy.

2. ____ There are a lot of buses on 88th Street.

3. ____ There are children on 88th Street.

4. ____ Cars are moving down 88th Street all night.

5. ____ There is the sound of music.

Making Inferences

If, in your opinion, the sentence is true, write "T." If, in your opinion, the sentence is false, write "F."

1. ____ It's winter in the story and it's cold.

2. ____ Bobby is in his apartment.

3. ____ It's 9:00 in the morning in the story.

4. ____ "Bang" is the sound of a door closing.

5. ____ "Click" is the sound of a siren.

Stating Facts

1. Give three examples of sounds on 88th Street.

   a. _____

   b. _____

   c. _____

2. Give four examples of kinds of music.

   a. _____

   b. _____

   c. _____

   d. _____

3. Give three examples of kinds of sirens.

   a. _____

   b. _____

   c. _____

   For more advanced students:

4. Give some examples of other kinds of noises on 88th Street.

   _____

Discussion Questions for More Advanced Students

Write or discuss the answers to the following questions:

1. Discuss one or two famous musicians from your country. Why are they so good? Describe their music.

2. Describe your street in your country. On a typical day, are there children? Cars? Garbage trucks? Are there people selling food? Animals? Music? How is it different from your neighborhood here in the United States?

3. Bring in some music from your country (a record or a tape). Play a little bit of it for the other students and explain it.

4. What sounds make you happy?

5. What noises drive you crazy?

VOCABULARY EXERCISES

Look at these words:

   an ambulance   the police   ✓ the fire department

Write the correct word in the sentences that follow.

1. Help! The sofa is burning! Quick! Call _the fire department_ .

2. What's that noise? Someone's trying to get in our apartment. Quick! Call _____ .

3. What's the matter with that old lady? Is she sick? Yes. Quick! Somebody call _____ .

Look at these words:

   opera   classical   rock

Write the correct word in the sentences below.

1. _____ is the music of young people. Sometimes it's fast and noisy.

2. _____ is a story with music.

3. _____ music is the music of men like Beethoven, Bach, and Tchaikovsky.

38

Select one of the following verbs and write it in the correct space:

is moving ✓is asking is giving
is coming in is closing

1. He *is asking* the girl a question.

2. She _____ the window.

3. He _____ the sofa.

4. He _____ the door.

5. She _____ her sister a present.

THE SOUNDS OF LIFE ON MY STREET

This is your story. Write the correct information about yourself in the empty spaces.

Sounds. The sounds of life on _____ (your street). There are the voices of _____ (who?). _____ (what are they saying?)

There are shouts of _____.

There are the calls of _____.

All day and all night there are the sounds of _____, and of _____, and of _____. All day and all night there are the noises of _____ and of _____. There are the noises of doors closing. Bang. Click.

39

There is also the sound of people talking. There is the strange sound of ———(language)——— , and there is the familiar sound of ——————my language. Sometimes I get a headache from all the noise.

7

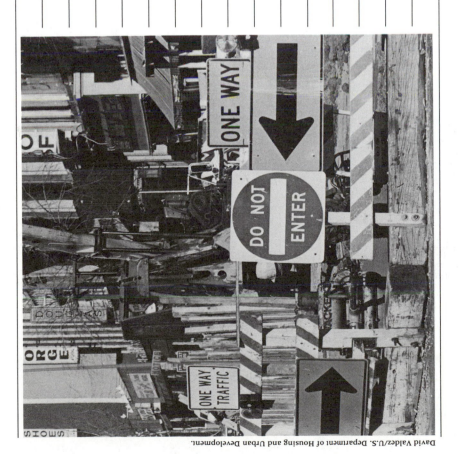

David Valdez/U.S. Department of Housing and Urban Development.

Before you read, answer these questions:

What are you doing now?

How do you feel? Are you happy, sad, tired, sleepy, so-so, fine, in good shape?

Where are you going after this class?

Is anyone waiting for you?

Say these words after your teacher or after an American friend:

		Phrases and expressions
go	ba′ by	have school
but	al′ most	leave ____ alone
please	some′ where	stay home
guy	tax′ i	listen to
dark	dri′ ver	

walk	a round′	wait for
feel	for get′	come back
home′ work	sud′ den ly	blow ____ 's horn
fi′ nal	to mor′ row	

As you read, think about these questions:

Where's Bobby going?

Is his mother happy about it?

Who's waiting for Bobby?

Why does Bobby feel tired when he's alone?

Bobby is at home. Someone is waiting for him, so he's going out. His mother is not happy about that.

unusual these days in the United States.

	U.S. Families with Children but No Husbands or Fathers in the Home	
	Number of families	Percentage of families
1960	1,891,000	7.4%
1970	2,926,000	10.2%
1980	5,445,000	17.6%

Is it the same in your country?

BOBBY, WHERE ARE YOU GOING?

Mother: Bobby, where are you going?

Bobby: Out.

Mother: Where?

Bobby: Around.

Mother: But it's eight o'clock, and you have school tomorrow.

Bobby: So what?

Mother: What about your homework?

Bobby: Forget it.

Mother: Bobby, please.

Bobby: Come on. I'm fourteen. Leave me alone.

Mother: Bobby, please stay home.

Bobby: I'm going out.

Mother: Bobby, listen to me. I'm your mother. You're *not* going out, and that's final.

Bobby: I'm not a baby. All the guys are out. They're waiting for me. Good-bye.

Mother: Bobby, Bobby, come back. What boys? Bobby? If only your father . . .

It's dark. The street is almost empty. Somewhere on Second Avenue a taxi driver is blowing his horn. Bobby is walking alone. It's only eight o'clock, but suddenly he feels tired, very tired.

Cultural facts

Families in the United States

Mrs. Curtis is both a mother and a father to Bobby. This is not so

COMPREHENSION EXERCISES

Finding the Facts

If the sentence is true, write "T." If the sentence is false, write "F."

1. ____ Bobby is staying home.

2. ____ Bobby is a baby.

3. ____ Bobby has school tomorrow.

4. ____ Bobby is walking alone at the end of the story.

5. ____ Bobby is feeling very good at the end of the story.

Making Inferences

If, in your opinion, the sentence is true, write "T." If, in your opinion, the sentence is false, write "F."

1. _____ It's morning in the story.

2. _____ It's Saturday.

3. _____ Bobby's mother is staying home that evening.

4. _____ Bobby is tired because it's late at the end of the story.

5. _____ Bobby's friends are waiting outside his apartment building.

Stating Opinions

Write or discuss the answers to the following questions:

1. What time is it in the story?
2. Why is Mrs. Curtis (Bobby's mother) upset?

Exercise for More Advanced Students: Stating Opinions

Write or discuss the answers to the following questions:

1. Why is Bobby going out?
2. Why is Bobby angry in the story?
3. Why is Bobby tired at the end of the story?

VOCABULARY EXERCISES

Select a verb and write it in the correct space:

is waiting for   is listening to
is coming back   is walking

1. He _____ to the bus stop.

2. He _____ the radio.

3. She _____ the bus.

4. He _____ to his apartment.

Synonyms

Select from the list the word that is similar to the words in the exercise. Write the synonym in the correct empty space.

final   *baby*   *guy*

1. the last _____

2. a man or boy _____

3. a very small child _____

Antonyms

Select from the list below the word that is the opposite of the words in the exercise. Write the antonym in the correct empty space.

forget   *go*   *empty*
stay   *leave alone*   *dark*

1. full _____

2. come back _____

3. light _____

4. remember _____

5. bother _____

6. leave _____

YOUR FEELINGS AND OPINIONS

Finish the following sentences any way that you want.

1. Bobby is _____

2. Bobby's mother is _____

3. Bobby isn't _____

4. All the guys are _____

5. A taxi driver is _____

6. Bobby's mother isn't _____

7. The street is _____

8. This story is _____

David Valdez/U.S. Department of Housing and Urban Development.

Before you read, answer these questions:

Who are you with now? Are you with your family? Your classmates? Are you alone?

When do you see your friends?

Think of boys in your country. Can they go out at night with their
friends? Can fourteen-year-old boys go out? How late can they
stay out? What about girls?

Say these words after your teacher or after an American friend:

		Phrases
watch	mo´ vie	get into trouble
can	par´ ty	What else?
think	mid´ night	get angry
home	week´ day	be all right
phone	pa´ rent	be in trouble
ring (v.)	sil´ ly	have a good time
wrong	fa´ ther	"be ____ fault"
dear	an´ swer	Thank you.
tell	un hap´ py	
love	tel´ e vi sion	
health	con ver sa´ tion	
laugh	im me´ di ate ly	

As you read, think about these questions:

Why is Mrs. Curtis upset?
Where is Bobby?
What time is it?
Is he coming home soon?

Bobby is out. His mother is at home. She's thinking about her son.

SHE'S WORRIED

It's so late, and he's out. Where is he? I'm sure he's with those boys.
Boys? They're not boys. They're four or five years older than Bobby.
Why, why is he out with them? I'm sure they're getting into trouble.
What else are they doing? I'm sure they're not at a movie or watching
television. They're probably at a party. But it's midnight, and it's a
weekday night. Where are their parents? That's a silly question. What
good are parents? Oh, I'm so worried I can't think. What can I do?
What can I do?

A few minutes later the phone rings . . .
Hello?
Bobby! Where are you?
But . . . but Bobby, it's 12:00.
Well, when *are* you coming home?
You . . . you're too young. You're still a child.
Now, Bobby, don't get angry. You are only fourteen.
Bobby? Is anything wrong?
Are you sure? Are you sure you're all right? You're not in trouble, are
  you?
What? You're coming home *when*?
Oh no. Dear, you can't. No.
Because I'm worried about you.
Who's that? Bobby, who are you with?
But . . . please tell me. You're *not* alone.
I'm glad you're having a good time. But . . . what about me? I'm here
  alone worrying about you.

47

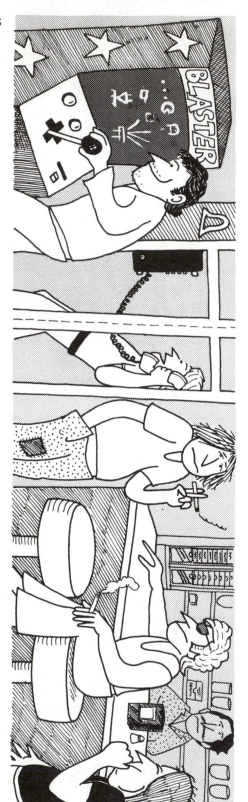

It's my fault. All day . . . at work. No father. It's my fault that you're unhappy. It's all my fault.

Well, thank you, dear.

Thank you. I love you, too.

Well, when are you coming home?

Think about your health. It's after 12:00. Bobby. Now, listen, listen. I'm getting angry, so come home this minute.

Listen to me. I'm your mother.

All right. I *am* listening to you.

Yes.

Yes.

Now, Bobby. It's too late for this conversation. So, this is final. Come home immediately . . . or don't come home at all.

Yes, that's right. Come home right now. Are you coming?

Bobby? Bobby? Answer me. . . .

There is no answer. The phone is dead. Bobby's mother is looking at her son's picture on the telephone table. In the picture Bobby is a baby. He's laughing.

Cultural facts

School in the United States

Children go to school from Monday to Friday. Sunday night through Thursday night are called "school nights," and most parents want their children to stay home after dinner and study.

Most children go to school from 8:30 A.M. to 2:30 P.M. They usually have homework to do each school night.

Is it the same in your country?

USDA photo.

COMPREHENSION EXERCISES

Finding the Facts

If the sentence is true, write "T." If the sentence is false, write "F."

1. ___ Bobby is at home at the end of the story.

2. ___ Bobby's friends are older than he is.

3. ___ Mrs. Curtis is very worried about her son.

4. ___ Bobby's father is at home.

5. ___ Bobby says he is coming home.

Making Inferences

If, in your opinion, the sentence is true, write "T." If, in your opinion, the sentence is false, write "F."

1. ___ Bobby loves his mother.

2. ___ Bobby is laughing at the end of the story.

3. ___ Mrs. Curtis is angry because Bobby is with his friends and she is alone.

4. ___ There is no answer in the final part of the conversation on the phone because Bobby is coming home immediately.

Discussion Exercises for More Advanced Students

Discuss the following questions with one or two classmates, or write the answers on another piece of paper.

1. Is Bobby a typical American teenager?
2. Is Mrs. Curtis a good mother?
3. Why are Bobby and his mother always having trouble?
4. In the story, Mrs. Curtis says, "What can I do? What can I do?" Tell her what to do.
5. Bobby is with his friends, but do you think he is alone, too? Can you be alone when you are with people? Is Mrs. Curtis alone? Give some examples of different ways that people can be alone.

6. Is it more difficult to be a child, a teenager, or an adult? Why? (Think carefully before answering.)

7. Why is the picture of Bobby as a baby important in the story?

VOCABULARY EXERCISES

Select the correct word from the list for each sentence. Write the word in the empty space.

listening to   immediately   ringing
laughing at   dead   conversation
✓ weekday

1. Tuesday night is a _weekday_ night.

2. My mother and sister are —————— music on the stereo.

3. Don't wait. Call the police ——————.

4. These flowers are no good. They're ——————.

5. Mr. and Mrs. Torres are having a serious ——————.

6. What's the matter? Are you —————— my English pronunciation or my grammar?

7. Answer the phone. It's ——————.

MY STORY

This is your story. Write the correct information about yourself in the empty spaces.

I'm tired. It's ——————. ————— is —————.
                    (time)   (your street)   (quiet? noisy? etc.)
I'm walking slowly through the streets to my ——————.
                                              (room? apart-
ment? etc.)
. I'm very tired.

I'm glad ——————————. I'm also glad
          (what are you glad about?)
——————. I'm not going to —————— tonight. That's
                          (a place)

good. Ah, home at last!

FREE READING

Look at this vocabulary:

dawn	hall	con fused'
cold	sleep	no' bo dy
gray	bed	Phrase
light	qui' et	at last
sky	eas' tern	
slow		

About five hours later:

88th Street is quiet. It's just about dawn, and there is a cold gray light in the eastern sky. Bobby is walking slowly through the empty streets to his home. He's tired and more confused than before.

He's glad there is nobody on the street. He's glad there is nobody in the hall or on the stairs. He's glad his mother is sleeping.

He's not going to school today, and that's final.

Ahh . . . bed at last.

For *Grammar Practice*, see page 185.

U.S. Department of Housing and Urban Development.

Before you read, answer these questions:

Do you have a landlord?
Do you rent the place where you live or do you own it?
Are there any apartments (houses, rooms) vacant near you?
Do you know anyone who is looking for an apartment or place to live?

Say these words after your teacher or after an American friend:

	Phrases and expressions
pet (n.)	Just a minute.
job	Let me see.
law	That's too bad.
show	have first choice
land' lord	be sorry
ten' ant	

va' cant   Thanks anyway.
qui' et   You're welcome.
cou' ple
tel' e phone
a vail' a ble

As you read, think about these questions:

Who is Mr. Fein?
Why is Mr. Torres calling him?
Why can't Mr. Torres' friends move into Apartment 5E?
Is Mr. Torres upset with Mr. Fein?

In this story, Carlos Torres is having a phone conversation with Louis Fein.

53

A PHONE CALL TO THE LANDLORD

Mrs. Fein: Hello?

Mr. Torres: Hello. Mr. Fein, please.

Mrs. Fein: Just a minute. Louis? Telephone.

Mr. Fein: Hello?

Mr. Torres: Mr. Fein?

Mr. Fein: Yes. Who's this?

Mr. Torres: This is Carlos Torres.

Mr. Fein: Who?

Mr. Torres: Carlos Torres. I'm one of your tenants at 228 88th Street.

Mr. Fein: Oh, sure. What's the problem?

Mr. Torres: No problem. I'm calling to ask a question.

Mr. Fein: Yes?

Mr. Torres: Apartment 5E is empty, right?

Mr. Fein: Wait a minute. Let me see. 5E. 228 88th Street. Vacant. Yes, that's right. It's empty.

Mr. Torres: Is it available?

Mr. Fein: Yes, for the right tenants.

Mr. Torres: What?

Mr. Fein: No pets, no more than four people, someone with a good job.

Mr. Torres: How many people?

Mr. Fein: Four.

Mr. Torres: My friends have three children.

Mr. Fein: How many adults?

Mr. Torres: Two.

Mr. Fein: No. That's five.

Mr. Torres: But one child is a baby.

Mr. Fein: I'm sorry. That's the law.

Mr. Torres: That's too bad. They're very nice, quiet people.

Mr. Fein: I'm sure they are. I'm sorry. Anyway, I'm showing the apartment to a young couple this afternoon. They have first choice.

Mr. Torres: Well, that's life. Thanks anyway.

Mr. Fein: You're welcome. Good-bye.

Mr. Torres: Good-bye.

Cultural facts

Apartments in the United States

There are lots of vacant apartments in the United States. It is easy to find one for rent. But it is difficult to find an inexpensive apartment in a nice building in a good location.

Is it the same in your country?

COMPREHENSION EXERCISES

Finding the Facts

If the sentence is true, write "T." If the sentence is false, write "F."

1. ___ Mr. Fein is a landlord.

2. ___ Mr. Torres is one of Mr. Fein's tenants.

3. ___ Apartment 5E is not available.

4. ___ Mr. Fein is showing 5E to Mr. Torres' friends this afternoon.

5. ___ Mr. Torres' friends have five children.

Making Inferences

If, in your opinion, the sentence is true, write "T." If, in your opinion, the sentence is false, write "F."

1. ___ Mr. Fein is married.

2. ___ Mr. Fein is looking for couples with no children.

3. ___ Mr. Torres is a good friend of Mr. Fein.

4. ___ Mr. Fein is angry at Carlos Torres for asking questions.

5. ___ Mr. Fein worries about the law.

Stating Facts

1. Tell me three things about Mr. Torres' friends.

   a. _____

   b. _____

   c. _____

2. The landlord is looking for families with:

   a. _____

   b. _____

   c. _____

Discussion Exercises for More Advanced Students

Write or discuss the answers to the following questions:

1. Tell the class some experiences you had when you rented an apartment, or tell the class some experiences a friend of yours had.

2. Tell the class some of the regulations you have to follow where you live.

3. Mr. Fein has trouble remembering names. What do you have trouble remembering? Why?

VOCABULARY EXERCISES

Synonyms

Select from the italicized words a synonym for each word numbered below.

    job   *couple*   *choice*

 √ *vacant*   *right*

1. empty ___ *vacant* ___

2. work _____

3. correct _____

4. husband and wife _____

5. selection _____

55

Antonyms

Select from the italicized words an antonym for each word numbered below.

no	*last*	✓*child*
right	*quiet*	*good-bye*
question	*young*	*tenant*

1. adult _child_
2. first _____
3. yes _____
4. hello _____
5. noisy _____
6. old _____
7. wrong _____
8. answer _____
9. landlord _____

YOUR STORY: REPORTING PROBLEMS TO THE LANDLORD

Read the following descriptions. Study the vocabulary.

There's no heat.

A window is broken.

There's no hot water.
There's no water.

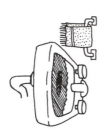

The stove isn't working.

A window is broken.

There's no hot water.
There's no water.

A pipe is leaking.

The stove isn't working.

The sink is blocked.
The sink is clogged.

The lights are out.
There is no electricity.

The faucet is leaking.

There's no air conditioning.

YOUR STORY

Imagine you are renting an apartment. Imagine you have a problem. Call your super and explain. Fill in the empty spaces that follow.

Super: Hello?

You: Hello. Is this _____? *(super's name)*

Super: Yes. Who's this?

You: This is _____. *(your name)*

Super: Who?

You: _____. I'm a tenant at _____. *(your name)* *(address)*

Super: Oh, sure. What's the matter?

You: I'm calling because _____. *(see the problems on page 56)*

Super: Oh, really?

You: Yes, it's terrible.

Super: Okay. Okay. When are you home?

You: I'm usually home after _____. But, when *(time)* are you coming?

Super: I'm busy tonight. How about tomorrow night at _____? *(time)*

You: Aren't you coming tonight?

Super: I'm busy.

You: Please, it's serious.

Super: What can I tell you?

You: Well, all right. But don't forget to come tomorrow.

Super: Sure. Sure. Good-bye.

You: Good-bye. See you tomorrow night.

57

10

MSEA Corning/U.S. Department of Housing and Urban Development.

Before you read, answer these questions:

Tell me about your building or house.
  What does it look like?
  Where is it?
Tell me about your apartment (room, house).
  What's it like?
  Is it large or small?
  How many rooms are there?
  Is it in good condition or run down?

Say these words after your teacher or after an American friend:

		Phrases and expressions
live	cry	What's _____ like?
small	so	be tired of
yet	hap' py	Wait a minute.
know	su' per	One thing at a time.
good	(superintendent)	be just looking
see	fol' low	be supposed to
come	noth' ing	Take your time.
knock	up stairs'	What's the matter?
door	beau' ti ful	
view (n.)	ex' er cise	
light	ex ci' ted	
cat	el' e va tor	
back		

As you read, think about these questions:

Where are John and Barbara living now?
Where are they going?

Which apartment is vacant?
Why is it so dark in the building?
Why is Barbara getting tired?
How does she feel at the end of the story?

John and Barbara Davis are a young couple. They are looking for their first apartment. They are walking to see an apartment now.

THEIR FIRST APARTMENT

Barbara: Now John, tell me. What's the apartment like? I'm so happy. I'm so tired of living with mother. I'm tired of her small apartment. She's my mother, but sometimes . . . . So, when are we moving? When?

John: Wait a minute, honey. One thing at a time. It isn't our apartment yet. We're just looking.

Barbara: I know, I know. But what's it like?

John: It's on the next block. Let's see. . . . It's small. The building is a little run down, and, as you can see, the neighborhood isn't very good. But . . . .

Barbara: Is the apartment vacant now?

John: Yes.

Barbara: I'm so happy. John, aren't you excited?

John: Yes, but . . . .

Barbara: We're almost there, aren't we?

John: Yes. This is the block.

Barbara: Oh, John. What a beautiful building!

John: No, dear, that's not our building.

Barbara: It's not?

John: No, this one. 228 88th Street. Mr. Fein is the landlord.

He's coming to see us at 11:30. The super's supposed to be here. (*John knocks on the door, and the super comes.*) Here he is.

The Super: Hello. Can I help you?

John: Hello. I'm John Davis. And this is my wife, Barbara.

Barbara: Hello.

The Super: Hello. You're here to see the apartment?

John: Yes.

The Super: Well, follow me upstairs. It's 5E. Take your time. (*He goes upstairs.*)

Barbara: The fifth floor? Is there a view?

John: I'm not sure.

Barbara: Where's the elevator? There's only one light in the hall!

John: Yeah, well . . . uh . . . there's no elevator.

Barbara: There isn't? Oh, well, climbing stairs is good exercise.

John: Mmmm.

Barbara: EEEEEK! What's that?

John: Oh, it's only a cat.

Barbara: I can't see. It's so dark.

John: Only three more floors to go.

Barbara: John . . . are you happy . . . happy that you're married?

John: What a silly question! Come on. Only two more floors to go now.

Barbara: I'm getting tired. Wait a minute.

John: We're almost there now. What's the matter. Aren't you feeling well?

Barbara: It's nothing.

John: Here we are. Our apartment is back there, I guess.

Barbara: Back there? At the back of the building?

John: Yes, I'm sorry. Wait a minute, Barbara. Wait and see the apartment. Maybe it's not so bad. Are you ready? (*He knocks and opens the door.*) Here it is. What do you think? Barbara? What's the matter? You're crying!

Cultural facts

Building Organization in the United States

In the United States, Apartment *101* is on the *first* floor of the building. Apartment *601* is on the *sixth* floor. Apartments 801, 802, and 803 are all on the eighth floor.

In some buildings, apartments have letters: 8A, 8B, 8C. All of these apartments are on the eighth floor.

In our story, there are only two apartments on each floor. Apartment 1*E* is the apartment on the east side of the first floor. Apartment 1*W* is on the west side of the first floor.

Is it the same in your country?

COMPREHENSION EXERCISES

Finding the Facts

If the sentence is true, write "T." If the sentence is false, write "F."

1. ___ Barbara is tired of John.

2. ___ The new apartment is on 88th Street.

3. ___ The new apartment is on the first floor.

4. ___ The apartment is in the back of the building.

5. ___ Barbara is laughing at the end of the story.

Circle the correct answer.

1. John and Barbara are looking for
   a. a cat.
   b. a neighborhood.
   c. an apartment.

2. The apartment is
   a. small.
   b. beautiful.
   c. tired.

3. Mr. Fein is the
   a. tenant.
   b. super.
   c. landlord.

4. In the hall, there is only one
   a. elevator.
   b. apartment.
   c. light.

5. The apartment is on the
   a. fifth floor.
   b. fourth floor.
   c. first floor.

6. At the end of the story, Barbara is
   a. getting tired.
   b. crying.
   c. moving.

Making Inferences

If, in your opinion, the sentence is true, write "T." If, in your opinion, the sentence is false, write "F." If you are

61

not sure, write "M" for maybe. Discuss your answers and your reasons for them with other students.

1. ___ Barbara is happy about living with her mother.

2. ___ John is very excited about the new apartment.

3. ___ Barbara's mother is living in a nice apartment.

4. ___ John is happy that he is married.

5. ___ John and Barbara do not have a lot of money.

Discussion Questions for More Advanced Students

Discuss the following questions with one or two classmates, or write the answers on another piece of paper.

1. Why is Barbara crying at the end of the story?
2. Is John happy he is married?
3. Is Barbara a good wife?
4. Does Barbara's mother have a lot of money?
5. Does Barbara know a lot about life? Does John?
6. Is it important to you to have a beautiful home to live in?
7. Discuss three things that are very important to you when you are looking for a place to live. Is a nice neighborhood important? A beautiful building? A large place? A lot of light? A nice view? A low rent? Nice neighbors? A place close to work or school?

VOCABULARY EXERCISES

Write the name of each object next to its picture.

    elevator   *light*

    cat   *stairs*

✓ *door*

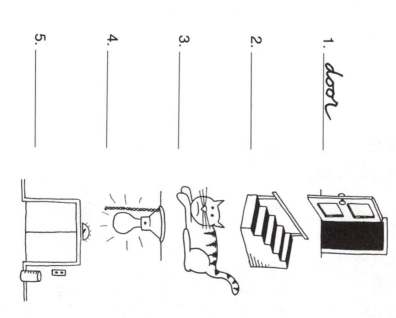

1. _door_

2. _____

3. _____

4. _____

5. _____

For More Advanced Students

Select the correct word and write it in the blank.

crying	beautiful	a little
living	landlord	√ super
walking	excited	

1. What are you doing?
   I'm calling the _super_.
   Why?
   There are no lights on the first floor.
2. Where's Ann these days?
   She's in Chicago.
   Alone?
   No, she's ———— with three other girls in an apartment.
3. What's the matter with Helen?
   She's ————.
   Why?
   Her boyfriend isn't coming to see her.
   Oh?
   Yes. She isn't very happy about it.
4. Carlos?
   Yes?
   Where are you going?
   To the baseball game in the park.
   Aren't you going early? It's only 12:00. ————.
   No, I'm not taking the bus, I'm ————.
   Good. That's good exercise.
5. Who's that girl?
   Marie Toussaint.
   She's ————.

6. What's the matter with you?
   I'm so ———— I can't work. I'm going home to Puerto Rico for a week.
   When?
   Tomorrow.
   Have a nice time.
7. What's the matter?
   I'm all right. I'm ———— tired. That's all.
   Are you sure?
   Yes.
8. What are you doing?
   Writing a check.
   To whom?
   To the ————, for our rent.
   Oh.

For *Grammar Practice*, see page 186.

PAR-NYC.

Before you read, answer these questions:

Are you happy with the condition of your apartment, room, or house?
When there is something wrong, do you fix it yourself?
Do people in your country like to do their own repairs?
Do you want to change anything in your home?
Are home repairs expensive?

Say these words after your teacher or after an American friend:

		Phrases and expressions
year	bath′ room	look around
cute	dan′ ger ous	Nice to see you again.
take	al read′ y	be careful of
low	i de′ a	
tip		

As you read, think about these questions:

Why is Mrs. Gold talking to Mr. Fein?
Does Mr. Fein want to talk to her?
What's the problem with Mrs. Gold's apartment?
What's dangerous in the building?
Why is the super too busy to come to Mrs. Gold's apartment?
Why is Mr. Fein in the building?

The next story is a conversation between Mrs. Gold and Mr. Fein. Mrs. Gold is not very happy with the condition of her building.

HELLO, MR. FEIN!

In the hall of 228 88th Street . . .

Mrs. Gold: Mr. Fein! Good morning. How are you today?

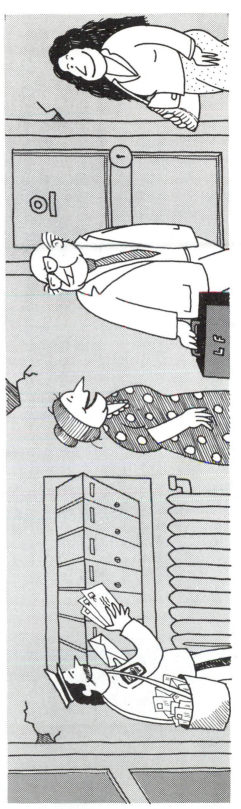

65

Mr. Fein: Fine, thanks. How are you? You're one of my oldest tenants, aren't you? About thirty-five years in the same apartment, am I right?

Mrs. Gold: Yes, that's right. What are you doing here?

Mr. Fein: I'm here to show 5E to a young couple.

Mrs. Gold: Oh, they're already upstairs with the super. They're looking around the apartment. They're a cute couple—so young.

Mr. Fein: Nice to see you again, Mrs. . . . .

Mrs. Gold: Take the elevator upstairs, Mr. Fein.

Mr. Fein: Is there an elevator in this building?

Mrs. Gold: No, but it's a good idea, isn't it?

Mr. Fein: We can't have elevators and low rents.

Mrs. Gold: Be careful of the stairs. They're dangerous.

Mr. Fein: Dangerous?

Mrs. Gold: They're dangerous because there are no lights.

Mr. Fein: There's always something.

Mrs. Gold: Oh, and Mr. Fein, my bathroom faucet is leaking.

Mr. Fein: Tell the super, that's what he's for.

Mrs. Gold: The super? The super's too busy to come when you have no money to tip him.

Mr. Fein: Nice to see you. (Thirty-five years. She's still the same. There's always something.)

Cultural facts

Tips in the United States

Many Americans do not like to tip people. They feel that workers should get a salary and not work for tips. Some workers *do* get tips regularly. These workers are: waiters and waitresses, taxicab drivers, bellhops, and, sometimes, maids in hotels, garage or parking-lot attendants, furniture movers, and other people who do not make a lot of money but do a good job for you.

Is it the same in your country?

COMPREHENSION EXERCISES

Finding the Facts

If the sentence is true, write "T." If the sentence is false, write "F."

1. ____ There is an elevator in the building.

2. ____ The young couple is upstairs.

3. ____ Mrs. Gold's bathroom faucet is okay.

4. ____ Mrs. Gold is a new tenant.

5. ____ The stairs are dangerous because they're old.

Making Inferences

If, in your opinion, the sentence is true, write "T." If, in your opinion, the sentence is false, write "F." If you are not sure, write "M" for maybe. Discuss your answers and your reasons for them with other students.

1. ____ Mrs. Gold knows the young couple.

2. ____ The super is busy all the time.

3. ____ The rent is low at 228 88th Street.

4. ____ The super is with the young couple now.

5. ____ The young couple are John and Barbara.

PAR-NYC.

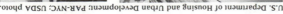

U.S. Department of Housing and Urban Development; PAR-NYC; USDA photo.

6. ____ Rents are sometimes more expensive in buildings with elevators.

7. ____ Mr. Fein goes to 228 88th Street very often.

Stating Facts

1. Tell me some new information about Mrs. Gold.

   a. _____

   b. _____

2. Tell me some new information about the building at 228 88th Street.

   a. _____

   b. _____

   c. _____

3. Write the answers to the following questions:

   a. Is Mr. Fein a young man? How do you know?

   b. Why is there no elevator? What does Mr. Fein say?

Exercise for More Advanced Students: Stating Opinions

Write or discuss the answers to the following questions:

1. Is Mr. Fein a good landlord?

2. Why is the super too busy to come to Mrs. Gold's apartment?

3. Why does Mr. Fein say, "There's always something?"

Summarizing

Choose four of the characters below. Write all you know about them.

Bobby	John	Mrs. Curtis
Mrs. Gold	Barbara	
Mr. Torres	Mr. Fein	

Predicting

Think about all of the characters and their stories. What do you think is going to happen? Write five things you think are going to happen. For example:

Mrs. Gold is going to meet John and Barbara.
Bobby is going to get into trouble.

Now you write five predictions.

1. _____

2. _____

3. _____

4. _____

5. _____

VOCABULARY EXERCISES

Fill-ins

Select the correct word and write it in the blank.

dangerous   careful
cute   low

1. Small babies are very _____.

2. $8.00 is a _____ price for a shirt nowadays in the United States.

3. Some streets in the city are _____.

4. Be _____ with your money when you are in a store.

Fill-ins for More Advanced Students

Select the correct word or phrase and write it in the blank.

looking around   tipping   taking   renting

1. Where are you going?
   I'm _____ the bus to 57th Street.

2. What are you doing?
   I'm _____.
   What for?
   My dictionary.
   It's not here. It's in the bedroom.

3. How much is the bill?
   $9.17.
   How much is my share?
   The hamburger—$3.50. The coke—75¢. $4.25 in all.
   Okay. How much are we _____ the waitress?
   $1.25. Give me 60¢.
   Here you are.

4. Where are you going? Are you moving?
   Yes. I am _____ an apartment near work.
   I'm sorry that you're going.
   Thanks, but we'll still be friends.

For *Grammar Practice*, see page 186.

12

U.S. Department of Housing and Urban Development.

Before you read, answer these questions:

Are apartments expensive in your town or city?

How much does an expensive apartment cost each month?

How much does an inexpensive apartment cost?

Where are the most beautiful apartments located? In what section of your town or city? Where are the cheapest ones located?

When do tenants usually have to pay their rent? What time of the month?

Say these words after your teacher or after an American friend:

	Phrases and expressions
stop	living room
find	be interested in
lease	have trouble
mo′ ment	have a problem
sun′ ny	

per′ fect

stan′ dard

bed′ room

bath′ room

kit′ chen

re mem′ ber

mag ni′ fi cent

Pleased to meet you.

How do you do?

take a look

As you read, think about these questions:

Are John and Barbara interested in Apartment 5E?

Is it an expensive apartment?

Is Mr. Fein in a hurry to rent Apartment 5E?

Are they going to take the apartment?

John, Barbara, and Mr. Fein are in Apartment 5E with the super, Armando. They are looking for a nice apartment to rent.

71

MEETING THE LANDLORD

Barbara: (*to John*) Dear? Someone's knocking at the door.

The Super: It's probably Mr. Fein. Look around some more. (*opening the door*) Hello, Mr. Fein. Come in.

Mr. Fein: Hello, Armando. Are they here?

Armando: Yes, they're in the living room.

Mr. Fein: What's their name again?

Armando: Davis.

Mr. Fein: Davis. That's right. I can never remember names. Davis.

Armando: I'm sure they're interested in the apartment.

Mr. Fein: Good. Thanks for showing them around.

Armando: Anytime. Anything else, Mr. Fein?

Mr. Fein: Not here. Stop and see the old lady in 1W. She's having some trouble.

Armando: Mrs. Gold? She always has a problem. Well, all right.

Mr. Fein: Thanks again, Armando.

Armando: Anytime. Good-bye.

Mr. Fein: (*to John and Barbara*) Hello? Hello, I'm Louis Fein. Are you Mr. David?

John: Mr. Davis. Hello, Mr. Fein. This is my wife, Barbara. Barbara, this is Mr. Fein.

Barbara: Pleased to meet you.

Mr. Fein: How do you do? Well, are you going to take it? It's a magnificent apartment. You have a living room, bedroom, bathroom, and kitchen. The rent is very low for this neighborhood. Take it right away. Two more couples are coming this afternoon. It's difficult to find an apartment for only $875.

Barbara: $875 a month? But . . . that's a lot!

Mr. Fein: Well, if you're not interested . . . I'm a busy man.

Apartment 5E, 228 88th Street

LEASE

1. Tenants must pay the rent on time.
2. Only tenants can live in the apartment.
3. Tenants can not use the apartment for business.
4. Tenants can not make changes in the apartment.
5. Tenants must take good care of the apartment.
6. The landlord is not responsible for any damage to the apartment.
7. The landlord must give the tenants:
   a. hot and cold running water.
   b. heat during the winter.
8. This lease is a two–year lease.
9. Tenants must give the landlord one month's rent in advance and one month's rent security.
10. No more than four people can live in this apartment.

RULES AND REGULATIONS

1. Children can not play in the halls.
2. Tenants must put garbage into the garbage cans on the street.
3. Tenants can not have a clothes washer, clothes dryer or dishwasher.
4. Tenants can not leave anything in the halls.
5. Tenants can not play musical instruments or make noise after 11:00 p.m.
6. Tenants can not keep animals in the apartment.

John: Wait a moment. Barbara, how about it?

Barbara: Well, the kitchen is nice. The living room is sunny. It's not perfect, John, but it's better than living with Mother.

John: Good. Can we see the lease?

Mr. Fein: Sure. Here. Take a good look. It's a standard lease.

Lease Vocabulary

		Phrases and expressions
must	busi′ ness	make changes in
pay	dam′ age	take care of
use	win′ ter	washing machine
clean	dish′ wash er	clothes dryer
month	out side′	be responsible for
play	max′ i mum	in advance
have	an′ i mal	garbage can
leave	se cur′ i ty	musical instrument
rule	reg u la′ tion	

Cultural facts

Housing in the United States

A *studio* or an *efficiency* is a small apartment. It has a kitchen, a living room, a bedroom, and a bathroom—all in one large room. A *one-bedroom* apartment has a kitchen, living room, bathroom, and bedroom. A *duplex* has rooms on two floors. A *duplex* is usually expensive to rent.

People who have the money can buy a *condominium* or *cooperative* apartment. They can be very expensive.

There are more private homes today in the United States than ever before:

1960	1970	1980
46,758,000	46,791,000	58,255,000

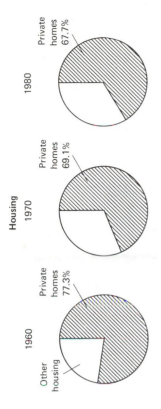

Housing

1960 — Other housing, Private homes 77.3%

1970 — Private homes 69.1%

1980 — Private homes 67.7%

But there are more people today, too. And many people do not have the money to buy a house.

Is it the same in your country?

COMPREHENSION EXERCISES

Finding the Facts

If the sentence is true, write "T." If the sentence is false, write "F."

1. ____ The super's name is Armando.

2. ____ John's last name is David.

3. ____ Mr. Fein cannot remember names very well.

4. ____ Mr. Fein says other people are interested in seeing Apartment 5E.

5. ____ Barbara thinks that Apartment 5E is perfect.

Making Inferences

If, in your opinion, the sentence is true, write "T." If, in your opinion, the sentence is false, write "F." If you are not sure, write "M" for maybe. Discuss your answers and your reasons for them with other students.

1. ____ Armando isn't interested in Mrs. Gold's problem.

2. ____ 5E is a magnificent apartment.

3. ____ Barbara is happy with the apartment.

4. ____ John and Barbara are probably going to take the apartment.

5. ____ Mr. Fein is not very interested in renting the apartment.

Finding the Facts

If the sentence is true, write "T." If the sentence is false, write "F."

1. ____ The landlord must give hot and cold running water.

2. ____ The tenants can invite other people to live with them.

3. ____ Tenants can keep a bicycle in the hall.

4. ____ Tenants can have dogs and cats.

5. ____ Tenants must put their garbage in the hall.

Making Inferences

If, in your opinion, the sentence is true, write "T." If, in your opinion, the sentence is false, write "F." If you aren't sure, write "M" for maybe. Discuss your answers and your reasons for them with other students. According to the Lease:

1. ____ The tenants can have parties all night.

2. ____ Tenants can have children.

3. ____ Tenants can have washing machines.

4. ____ Three tenants can live in 5E.

5. ____ Children must play in the street or in the apartment.

Written Comprehension Questions

Write the answers to the following questions:

1. Who's knocking at the door?
2. What is John's last name?
3. Where's the super going at the end of the dialogue?
4. How much is the rent for 5E?
5. How many rooms are there in the apartment?
6. Why is the apartment good (in Barbara's opinion)?

7. Why isn't the apartment perfect?
8. Why do you think John likes the apartment?
9. Do you think Mr. Fein shows John and Barbara a *standard* lease? Why or why not?
10. Are John and Barbara going to rent the apartment? Why or why not?

Comprehension Questions for Students Who Have an Apartment Lease

Look at your lease and answer these questions as well as you can.

1. Do you have a standard lease?
2. Can you have a business in your apartment?
3. Can you have pets in your apartment?
4. Can you have a piano?
5. Can you have a dishwasher in your apartment?
6. Can you play music anytime during the day or night?
7. Must new tenants give the landlord rent in advance? If so, how much? One month's rent? Two month's rent?
8. Must new tenants give the landlord security? If so, how much?
9. Can children play in your building?
10. Can children live in your building?
11. Must you give the super extra money to get an apartment in your building (key money)?
12. Is your rent high or low for your neighborhood?
13. How long is your lease?
14. What does your lease say you cannot do in your apartment?
15. When is your rent due? On the last day of the month? On the first of the month? When?

Some Questions for Students Who Do Not Have an Apartment Lease

Write the answers to the following questions or discuss them with your classmates.

1. Why don't you have a lease? Do you have a mortgage? Do you rent but have no lease? Do you live in a school dormitory?
2. Do you have rules and regulations that you must follow? If so, list five of them below:
   a. _____
   b. _____
   c. _____
   d. _____
   e. _____
3. What's nice about the place where you live?
4. Is there anything that's not so nice about the place where you live?
5. How long do you plan to live in this place?

For *Grammar Practice*, see page 188.

13

U.S. Department of Housing and Urban Development.

Before you read, answer these questions:

Imagine that you are looking for an apartment. Imagine also that you have $2,000 for rent, security, and moving expenses. Now answer these questions.

What are you looking for in an apartment? A good location? A quiet apartment? A good kitchen? A lot of space? A good view? Cheap rent? Good closets? Air conditioning? What? How much are you ready to pay for rent? Where do you want to find an apartment? What part of the city are you going to look in?

Say these words after your teacher or after an American friend:

		Phrases and expressions
sign	ev′ ery	air conditioner
dog	e nough′	After you.
key	a gain′	Of course.
paint	laun′ dro mat	
get	de ci′ sion	
laun′ dry	cur′ rent	

As you read, think of these questions:

What do John and Barbara decide to do about the apartment?
Why does John give the landlord a check?
Why isn't Mr. Fein interested in answering their questions?
What do they want to know about the apartment?
Do John and Barbara leave with Mr. Fein?

The story is a conversation between John and Barbara Davis and Mr. Fein, the landlord. They are still in apartment 5E.

SOME QUESTIONS

Mr. Fein: Well, what's your decision?
John: When can we sign the lease?
Mr. Fein: Can you pay me the security and the rent now?
John: Yes.
Mr. Fein: Good. Sign here.
Barbara: How much is the rent again?
Mr. Fein: $875 for the rent. $875 for the security. That's $1,750 in all.
Barbara: $1,750 . . . John?
John: That's fine. Can I give you a check?
Mr. Fein: Sure.
John: Here you are.

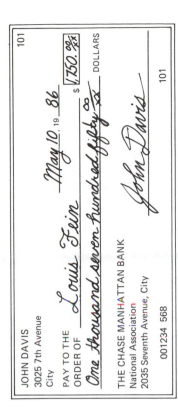

JOHN DAVIS
3025 7th Avenue
City   101

PAY TO THE
ORDER OF *Louis Fein*   *May 10* 19 *86* $ *1,750.00*

One thousand seven hundred fifty xx   DOLLARS

THE CHASE MANHATTAN BANK
National Association
2035 Seventh Avenue, City   *John Davis*

001234 568   101

Mr. Fein: Any questions?

Barbara: Yes. Just a few. Where can I do the laundry?

Mr. Fein: There's a laundromat in the neighborhood.

John: Can we have an air conditioner?

Mr. Fein: There's not enough current for a large one. This is an old building.

John: Can we have a dog?

Barbara: A cat?

Mr. Fein: No, no pets at all.

Barbara: Who are our neighbors?

Mr. Fein: The old lady in 1W can answer all your questions. Come with me.

John: Okay. But I have one more question. When can we move in?

Mr. Fein: On the first of the month. You have the keys. Ready to go?

Barbara: Oh, yes . . . one more question. Can you paint the apartment?

Mr. Fein: Sure. It's the law to paint an apartment every three years or with each new tenant. After you, Mrs. Daniel.

John: Davis. Can we get some lights on the stairs. It's dangerous.

Mr. Fein: That's the super's job. Tell Armando about it. Let's go.

Barbara: Can we stay here for a few minutes?

Mr. Fein: Oh . . . of course. Sure. Well good-bye.

John: Good-bye. Thank you.

Barbara: Good-bye.

John: (after Mr. Fein leaves) Are you going to cry?

Barbara: Maybe.

John: Again?

Cultural facts

Rent in the United States

It is not unusual today to pay $800 a month or more for a nice apartment. Many people pay 40 percent of their salary for housing.

Is it the same in your country?

COMPREHENSION EXERCISES

Finding the Facts

If the sentence is true, write "T." If the sentence is false, write "F."

1. _____ The rent is $875 a month.

2. _____ They can have a dog.

3. _____ Landlords must paint apartments every two years.

4. _____ Barbara's last name is Daniel.

5. _____ John can pay by check.

Making Inferences

If, in your opinion, the sentence is true, write "T." If, in your opinion, the sentence is false, write "F." If you are not sure, write "M" for maybe. Discuss your answers and your reasons for them with other students.

1. _____ Barbara does not know how much money they have.

2. _____ John does not have any questions to ask Mr. Fein.

3. _____ Mr. Fein is not interested in talking to John and Barbara.

4. _____ Mr. Fein does not know the law.

5. _____ Barbara is unhappy about renting 5E.

Written Comprehension Questions

Answer the following questions in the spaces below.

1. When can John sign the lease?

_____

2. How much is the rent?

_____

3. How much is the security?

_____

4. Who are John and Barbara's neighbors?

_____

5. When can John and Barbara move in?

_____

More Difficult Written Comprehension Questions

Write the answers to the following questions in the spaces below.

1. How much work does Mr. Fein do in his building?

_____

2. Do you think Mr. Fein is going to paint the apartment?

_____

3. Are John and Barbara going to have trouble with the apartment? Why or why not?

_____

4. Is Mr. Fein happy to say good-bye. Why or why not?

_____

Discussion

Look back at the story on page 77. You can see in the story that it is a good idea to ask questions before you rent an apartment. Think of some good questions that people might ask when they rent an apartment. Write ten of them here.

1. _____

2. _____

3. _____

4. _____

5. _____

6. _____

7. _____

8. _____

9. _____

10. _____

Discussion Topics for More Advanced Students

Select one student to be the landlord. Select another student to be the person who is looking for an apartment. Then practice the following situations:

Situation #1

The apartment: It's cheap, but it's in bad condition.
The landlord: You don't want to repair the apartment.
The person who is looking: You like the apartment very much, but you don't want the landlord to know you like it. You want him to repair the apartment.

Situation #2

The apartment: It's not good and not bad.
The landlord: You're in a hurry. You want to go home.
The person who is looking: You want more information about the apartment, your neighbors, and so on.

Situation #3

The apartment: It's okay.

The landlord: You want to rent the apartment very much.

The person who is looking: You think the apartment is okay. But you know that there is another empty apartment in the same building. You want to see that one, too.

Situation #4

The apartment: It's too expensive, but it's large and beautiful.

The landlord: You want to rent the apartment.

The person who is looking: You can't rent this apartment, but you want to make a good impression on the landlord. You want him to call you when he has a smaller, cheaper apartment.

VOCABULARY EXERCISE

Select the correct word for the blank. Each word may be used one or more times.

   paint   move in   key

   sign   ✓pay   laundromat

Example: (*In a restaurant*)

Customer: Excuse me. Can I have my check?

   Server: Yes.

Customer: Do I ___pay___ you?

   Server: No. ___Pay___ at the door.

Tenant: This apartment is good.

Landlord: Are you going to take it?

Tenant: Yes. Where's the lease?

Landlord: Here. Read it and _____ it.

Tenant: Can I use your pen?

Landlord: Here you are.

Tenant: When can we _____? We're in a hotel now.

Landlord: Today's the 15th. The apartment isn't ready.

Tenant: It isn't?

Landlord: No. You can _____ next week.

Tenant: The sooner, the better.

Landlord: The apartment's in perfect condition.

Tenant: Oh, no, it isn't. Please _____ it before we move in.

Landlord: Who, me?

Tenant: It's the law, isn't it?

Landlord: Maybe. Well, because you're so nice. I'm
going to paint it white.

Tenant: Thanks. That's fine.

John: Open the door.

Barbara: I can't.

John: Why not?

Barbara: I can't find the _____.

Tenant: Where can I find a _____?

Landlord: There's one on 89th Street.

Tenant: Do they have washers and dryers?

Landlord: Yes, everything.

14

U.S. Department of Housing and Urban Development.

Before you read, answer these questions:

Describe someone you know.

What is he or she to you? Your friend, wife, husband, or brother?

How old is this person?

How tall? Is this person tall, average height, or short?

Is this person fat, average weight, or thin?

What color is this person's hair and eyes?

What does this person do for a living?

Say these words after your teacher or after an American friend:

grade	eye	boy' friend
class	long	of' fice
bank	black	mar' riage
tall	like	T' V'
short	free	na' tion al

blond	say	at trac' tive	have a date
hair	typ' ist	un' at trac tive	
brown	stu' dent	in de per' dent	
green	hea' vy		

Phrases and expressions

elementary school

light _____ (color)

_____ own

As you read, think about these questions:

What does Emily do for a living?

What does Helen do for a living?

Do they like their jobs?

Do they go out a lot?

Do Emily and Helen want to get married?

Are they happy with their lives?

The next story is about two single women. They live in apartment 3W in the same building as Mrs. Gold.

THE SINGLE WOMEN IN 3W

There are two single women in apartment 3W. One woman's name is Emily Gibson and the other's name is Helen Rhodos. Emily is an elementary school teacher. She has a first-grade class this year. Helen is a typist at the First National Bank.

Emily is twenty-eight years old. She isn't tall or short; she isn't attractive or unattractive. She has blond hair. Well, it isn't really blond. It's almost brown. She has light green eyes. Emily is very quiet at parties. She is happiest in her classroom because her students are like her own children.

Helen is younger than Emily. She is twenty-six years old, short, and a little heavy. She has long black hair and brown eyes. Helen is usually quiet, but she isn't as quiet as Emily. Emily and Helen are busy during the day, but in the evenings they often have nothing to do. It is difficult for quiet women to meet men in the city. They do not like to go out alone and walk around because the city can be dangerous at night. They do not go out unless they have someplace to go. So Helen and Emily usually stay home in 3W at night.

Sometimes on the weekends they have dates. Helen has a boyfriend from her office. She has a date with him once or twice a month. But as Emily is always saying, "Dates aren't everything. Marriage isn't everything. I have my friends and my job. I'm free to come and go anytime. I'm happy to be independent now. But maybe. . . . "

Cultural facts

Marriage in the United States
More than 40 percent of American women are not married or living with a husband.

	Women 18–44 Years Old (1980)
Women who are married and are living with their husbands	27,652,000
Women who are married and are not living with their husbands	1,934,000
Women who are widowed or divorced	4,069,000
Women who are single	12,270,000

Is it the same in your country?

COMPREHENSION EXERCISES

Cloze Exercise

Read the original story again. The following exercise is a little different. Every fifth word is missing. Fill in the blanks with a word—just *one* word. It's not necessary to write the same word that is in the story. But you must write a word that is correct in grammar and in content. For example:

There are two single ———— in apartment 3W.

You can answer *girls* or *women*. But *men* is not correct because al'' the pronouns in the story are *she*. Okay? You also cannot write *girl* or *woman* because *two* is plural. You must write *girls* or *women*. Now try to fill in the blanks.

There are two single ———— in apartment 3W.

One ———— name is Emily Gibson ———— the other's name is ———— Rhodos. Emily is an ———— school teacher. She has ———— first-grade class this ————. Helen is a typist ———— the First National Bank.

———— is twenty-eight years old. ———— isn't tall or short; ———— isn't attractive or un-attractive. ———— has blond hair. Well, ———— isn't really blond. It's ———— light ———— eyes. Emily is very ———— at parties. She is ———— in her classroom because ———— students are like her ———— chil-dren. Helen is younger ———— Emily. She is ————

twenty-six ———— old, short, and a ———— heavy. She has long ———— hair and brown eyes. ———— is usually quiet, but ———— isn't as quiet as ————. Emily and Helen are ———— during the day, but ———— the evenings they often ———— nothing to do. It ———— dif-ficult for quiet women ———— meet men in the ————. They do not like ———— go out alone and ———— around because the city

be dangerous at night. _____ do not go out _____ they have someplace to _____. So Helen and Emily _____ stay home in 3W _____ night.

Sometimes on the weekends _____ have dates. Helen has _____ boyfriend from her office. _____ has a date with _____ once or twice a _____.

But as Emily is _____ saying, "Dates aren't everything. _____ isn't everything. I have _____ friends and my job. _____ free to come and _____ anytime. I'm happy to _____ independent now. But maybe . . ."

Finding the Facts

If the sentence is true, write "T." If the sentence is false, write "F."

1. ____ Emily is a teacher.
2. ____ The women live in 2W.
3. ____ Helen is a typist.
4. ____ Emily is 28 years old.
5. ____ Helen is 24 years old.
6. ____ Emily is happiest when she is at a party.
7. ____ Helen is as quiet as Emily.
8. ____ The women like to go out alone at night.
9. ____ They have dates every weekend.
10. ____ Helen has a boyfriend.

Making Inferences

If, in your opinion, the sentence is true, write "T." If, in your opinion, the sentence is false, write "F." If you are not sure, write "M" for maybe. Discuss your answers and your reasons for them with other students.

1. ____ Emily has a boyfriend.
2. ____ Helen and Emily are worried about the future.
3. ____ Helen and Emily don't have many dates.
4. ____ Emily is happy with her job.
5. ____ Helen has only one boyfriend.

Discussion Questions

Write or discuss the answers to the following questions.

1. What floor is their apartment on?
2. When are Helen and Emily busy?

3. When is Emily very quiet?

4. Why don't they like to go out alone?

5. Who has a date once or twice a month?

Discussion Questions for More Advanced Students

Write or discuss the answers to the following questions.

1. Why do you think that people like Emily are quiet at parties?

2. Why do people like Helen and Emily spend so many evenings alone?

3. Emily says, "I'm happy to be independent now." Then she says, "But maybe . . ." Finish her sentence: But maybe _____

4. Emily says, "Marriage isn't everything." What's your opinion?

5. Is it good for young people to live alone? Why or why not? What about young women?

6. Is it good for young people to be free to come and go anytime? Why or why not? What about young women?

7. Describe a beautiful woman from your country. Is she tall? Is she thin? Is she blond? Does she have long hair? Does she have big eyes?

8. When do you think most people are happiest? When are you happiest?

9. Are you usually quiet? Why or why not?

10. Describe a typical date in the United States. Where do people go? What do they do? How much money does it cost?

11. Describe a typical date in your country. How is it different from an American date?

VOCABULARY EXERCISES

Synonyms

Select from the italicized words a synonym for each word numbered below.

usually   free   boyfriend

1. most of the time _____

2. independent _____

3. regular date _____

Antonyms

Select from the italicized words an antonym for each word numbered below. Select the word that is the opposite.

happy *attractive* *long*
noisy *day* *short*

1. unattractive _____

2. quiet _____

3. tall _____

4. unhappy _____

5. night _____

6. short _____

For *Grammar Practice*, see page 189.

15

David Valdez/U.S. Department of Housing and Urban Development.

Before you read, answer these questions:

Think of a normal day in your life. Don't think about special or inter-esting days. Think about a normal Tuesday. Okay?

Now use your imagination! It's Tuesday. It's 7:00 in the morning. What are you doing?

Now it's 10:00 A.M. Where are you? What are you doing? It's noon. Now what's happening? Now it's 4:00. Are you doing anything different? Tell me about what you are usually doing at 6:00 P.M. and 9:00 P.M.

That's Tuesday. Is Wednesday different? What about the rest of the days in the week? Are most days in your life the same or very different?

Say these words after your teacher or after an American friend:

		Phrases and expressions
sit	make′ up	drive _____ crazy
then	dir′ ty	get out of
read	pro′ mise	get younger
act	ex plain′	be bored
strange	to night′	around the corner
hour	ex cuse′	be called
pic′ ture	type′ wri ter	in front of
tea′ cher	ab so lute′ ly	get dressed
		put on
		Prince Charming
		look for an excuse

As you read, think of these questions:

What is Helen tired of?
What does she want to do?
How does Emily feel?
What does Emily promise to do?

The conversation that follows is between Emily and Helen. They are at home. Helen is unhappy.

LET'S GO SOMEPLACE

Helen: I'm tired of sitting here night after night. I'm tired of looking at TV.

Emily: Then read a book.
Helen: Come on!
Emily: Why not?
Helen: Reading a book, looking at TV . . . they're the same. We're always home. Every night. The same four walls, the same pic-tures. It's driving me crazy.
Emily: What else can we do?
Helen: Well, we can go someplace.
Emily: Where?
Helen: Anywhere. Anything to get out of this apartment. We're never going to meet anyone if we're here all the time. We're not getting any younger, Emily.

Emily: Stop worrying.

Helen: I'm not worried. I'm bored.

Emily: You're acting so strange. What's really the matter?

Helen: Well, it's difficult to explain. It's only that . . . well . . . it's different for you, maybe. But from 9:00 to 5:00 every day . . . every single day, Emily . . . I'm at the same typewriter. And Emily, I'm twenty-six.

Emily: That's nothing. I'm twenty-eight.

Helen: But you're a teacher. Your job is interesting.

Emily: No job is interesting all the time.

Helen: Listen. Let's not argue. There's a place around the corner. It's called "Irene's." There are always lots of interesting people there at night. And where are we? Here . . . in front of the TV. Come on. It isn't too late. Get dressed. Put on some makeup. Maybe we can meet some men there.

Emily: Tomorrow, Helen. It's too late now.

Helen: Tomorrow? It's *always* tomorrow. We can go for just an hour. Please, Emily. Come with me. I can't go alone.

Emily: I can't.

Helen: Why not?

Emily: My hair . . . it's dirty.

Helen: We're not going to meet Prince Charming.

Emily: I can't. Friday. Let's go Friday.

Helen: What about *tonight?* Come on. You're just looking for an excuse.

Emily: No, really. Let's go Friday night.

Helen: Promise?

Emily: Yes . . . absolutely . . . Friday night . . . "Irene's."

Helen: Well, okay. Don't forget. Friday night and no excuses!

Cultural facts

Television in the United States

What do most Americans do in the evening? They watch TV.

In 1982, 98 percent of American homes had a TV. There are more than 150,000,000 TVs in the United States. Most Americans watch TV 6.7 hours every day.

Is it the same in your country?

COMPREHENSION EXERCISES

Finding the Facts

If the sentence is true, write "T." If the sentence is false, write "F."

1. ____ Helen is tired of watching TV.

2. ____ Helen is bored.

3. ____ Helen is worried about meeting a nice man.

4. ____ Emily is 28.

5. ____ Emily is a teacher.

6. ____ Emily thinks her job is interesting all the time.

7. ____ Helen is at the same typewriter from 9:00 to 5:00.

8. ____ Helen's hair is dirty.

9. ____ "Irene's" is a place around the corner from 228 88th Street.

10. ____ Emily promises to go to "Irene's" on Friday.

Making Inferences

If, in your opinion, the sentence is true, write "T." If, in your opinion, the sentence is false, write "F." If you are not sure, write "M" for maybe. Discuss your answers and your reasons for them with other students.

1. ____ Helen is tired of her life.

2. ____ Emily isn't going to "Irene's" because she's a teacher.

3. ____ Emily is not interested in meeting men.

4. ____ Emily is not really interested in going to "Irene's."

5. ____ They're going to go out to a movie on Friday.

6. ____ "Irene's" is probably a restaurant or a bar.

Stating Facts

1. Tell me two new things you now know about Helen from this story.

a. _____

b. _____

2. Tell me two new things you now know about Emily from this story.

a. _____

b. _____

3. Give three reasons why Helen wants to go to "Irene's."

a. _____

b. _____

c. _____

Remembering the Facts

Reread the story on page 91. Read it carefully to remember details. After that, read this and circle the correct word in each sentence. Do not look back at the original story when you are selecting the correct words.

Helen: I'm tired of (*working sitting laughing*) here night after night. I'm tired of looking at (*TV food the radio*).

Emily: Then read a book!

Helen: Come on!

Emily: Why not?

Helen: Reading a book, looking at TV . . . they're the same. We're always (*at work home at church*). Every night. The same four walls, the same pictures. It's driving me (*crazy happy tired*).

Emily: What else can we do?

Helen: Well, we can go (*someone sometime someplace*).

Emily: Where?

Helen: Anywhere. Anything to (*stay in come back to get out of*) this apartment. We're never going to meet (*anyone anyplace anytime*) if we are here all the time. We're not getting any (*older younger taller*), Emily.

Emily: Stop worrying.

Helen: I'm not worried. I'm (*tired bored happy*).

Emily: You're acting so strange. What's really the matter?

Helen: Well, it's difficult to (*talk write explain*). It's only that ... well ... it's different for you, maybe. But from 9:00 to 5:00 every day ... every single day, Emily ... I'm at the same typewriter. And Emily, I'm twenty-six.

Emily: That's nothing. I'm twenty-eight.

Helen: But you're a (*secretary typist teacher*). Your job is interesting.

Emily: No job is interesting all the time.

Helen: Listen. Let's not (*talk argue go*). There's a place around the corner. It's called "Irene's." There are always lots of interesting people there at night. And (*who where why*) are we? Here ... in front of the TV. Come on. It isn't too late. Get (*out dressed clothes*). Put on some makeup. Maybe we can meet some men there.

Emily: Tomorrow, Helen. It's too (*much early late*) now.

Helen: Tomorrow? It's *always* tomorrow. We can go for just an hour. Please, Emily. Come with me. I can't go (*alone single solo*).

Emily: I can't.

Helen: Why not?

Emily: My hair ... it's (*clean long dirty*).

Helen: We're not going to meet (*a doctor a man Prince Charming*).

Emily: I can't. Friday. Let's go Friday.

Helen: What about *tonight?* Come on. You're just looking for (*a prince an excuse a TV*).

Emily: No, really. Let's go Friday night.

Helen: Promise?

Emily: Yes . . . absolutely . . . Friday night . . . "Irene's."

Helen: Well, okay. Don't forget. Friday night and no excuses!

Written Comprehension Questions

Write the answers to the following questions:

1. Why is Helen bored?
2. Why isn't Emily interested in going to "Irene's"?
3. Why do you think that Helen isn't interested in going to "Irene's" alone?
4. Do you think Emily is going to "Irene's" with Helen on Friday?
5. Why do you think Emily and Helen have difficulty in meeting men?

Discussion Questions

1. What are you tired of? Give several answers, if possible.
2. Why are you tired of the things in number 1?
3. Can you do anything to change your life? What can you do?

VOCABULARY EXERCISES

Select the correct verb from the list and write it in the blank space.

sitting	explaining
acting strange	arguing
	putting on
	getting dressed

1. He's —————.

2. He's ————— his hat because he's going to work.

3. Read this dialogue:

He: I'm right.
She: No, you're wrong.
He: No, I'm not.
She: Yes, you are.
They're —————.

4. Read this dialogue:

She: What's a *lease*?
He: It's a contract.
She: For what?
He: For an apartment.
He's ————— a lease to her.

5. It's 7:00 and he's —————.

6. Read this dialogue:

She: What's the matter with that guy?

He: Which one?

She: The one who's _____.

He: Yeah, he looks crazy. I don't know what his problem is.

Select the correct word or words from the list and write it/them in the blank spaces.

bored	Friday	✓typewriter
is called	dirty	tonight
driving me crazy		

1. She's typing a letter on her *typewriter*.

2. Today is Thursday. Tomorrow is _____.

3. He's not interested. He's _____.

4. She's washing her hands because they're _____.

5. Stop that noise. It's _____.

6. I'm studying _____ because I'm going out tomorrow night.

7. His name is William, but he _____ "Red" by his friends.

For *Grammar Practice*, see page 192.

97

16

David Valdez/U.S. Department of Housing and Urban Development.

Before you read, answer these questions:

Do you know where there are singles' bars or singles' nightclubs
in your town?
Do you ever go there?
How do you meet people in these places?
Who makes the first move—the men or the women?

Say these words after your teacher or after an American friend:

	Phrases and expressions	
drink	over there	Cool it.
real	good-looking	No way.
fat	You can't win 'em all.	go on
both	Be cool.	Have it your way.
lo' ser	be worth	get going
bar' ten der		
ter rif' ic		

As you read, think of these questions:

Who do the men see in the bar?
What do the women look like?
Who are the women?
How do the men feel about the women?
Do they go over and meet the women?

The next dialogue is a conversation between two young men in a bar.
Read the story to see what these two men are talking about on this
Friday night at the bar.

LET'S FIND SOME GIRLS

Man # 1: Look at those girls.
Man # 2: Which ones?

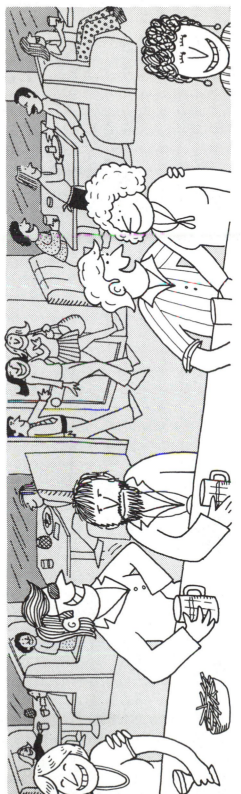

99

Man # 1: Those two over there.

Man # 2: At the end of the bar?

Man # 1: Yes, them.

Man # 2: You're not serious.

Man # 1: Yes. The two at the end of the bar.

Man # 2: Come on. They're losers.

Man # 1: Well, are there any others?

Man # 2: They aren't even worth a drink.

Man # 1: You're right, but there's nobody else around.

Man # 2: Let's wait.

Man # 1: Okay, but I'm getting tired of standing here and drinking.

Man # 2: Me, too. But take it easy. Be cool.

Man # 1: Hey! Look at those two beautiful girls at the door.

Man # 2: Hey! They are good-looking.

Man # 1: Let's go.

Man # 2: Oh, no. Cool it.

Man # 1: Why? They're terrific.

Man # 2: Yeah. So are their dates.

Man # 1: Oh, well, you can't win 'em all. There are still the two at the bar.

Man # 2: Oh, them.

Man # 1: They're terrible, yeah. But come on. It's only for one night, and it's getting late.

Man # 2: I'm tired of waiting, too. Which one is yours?

Man # 1: The short one with the long hair.

Man # 2: No way. She's for me.

Man # 1: Oh yeah?

Man # 2: Yeah. You take the blond.

Man # 1: Thanks a lot. You're a real friend.

Man # 2: Come on. Take the blond.

Man # 1: Forget it. I'm not interested. I'm going to have another drink. The bartender is looking this way. Go on. You can have both of them.

Man # 2: All right, all right. Have it your way. You can have the fat one, okay?

Man # 1: Okay. Let's get going.

Man # 2: (to the girls) Hello, girls. . . .

Cultural facts

Bars in the United States

More men than women go to bars. There were 61,200 bars in the United States in 1982. Most men go to bars to relax, talk to friends, and watch sports on the TV in the bar.

In the 1960s a new kind of bar was born—the singles' bar. This is a bar for young people (under 50) who want to meet other singles. Both males and females go there in the evening—usually between 9:00 P.M. and 1:00 A.M.

Is it the same in your country?

COMPREHENSION EXERCISES

Finding the Facts

If the sentence is true, write "T." If the sentence is false, write "F."

1. ___ The two men are at the bar.

2. ___ Two girls at the door are attractive.

3. ___ The two beautiful girls have dates with them.
4. ___ The shorter girl has long dark hair.
5. ___ The other girl has red hair.

Making Inferences

If, in your opinion, the sentence is true, write "T." If, in your opinion, the sentence is false, write "F." If you are not sure, write "M" for maybe. Discuss your answers and your reasons for them with other students.

1. ___ Only the two men and the bartender are at the bar.
2. ___ The men are in the bar because they are looking for girls.
3. ___ One of the girls at the bar is more attractive than the other in the men's opinion.
4. ___ The men aren't really interested in the girls at the bar.

Discussion Questions

Answer the following questions orally or write your answers on another piece of paper.

1. What do you think of the men in the story? Are all men like that when they are single and with their friends? What did you like about them? What didn't you like? Give examples.
2. What are the men looking for? What do you think they really want?

Discussion Questions for More Advanced Students

Answer the following questions orally or write your answer on another piece of paper.

1. What kind of attitude do the men have toward the women? Do you feel that their attitude is typical of all men or just American men?
2. How do you feel about the men? Are they sincere in what they say or do you think they are putting on an act for each other?

VOCABULARY EXERCISES

Matching

Draw a line from the word on the left to the word on the right that is the antonym (opposite) of the first word.

good-looking	dark
forget	tired of
interested in	unattractive
light	remember

Using Vocabulary

Answer the following questions:

1. Are you tired of English or interested in English?
2. Is your best friend's hair light or dark?
3. Are movie actors usually attractive or unattractive?
4. Is the woman in this picture good-looking or unattractive?

PAR-NYC.

5. Are American cars good-looking or unattractive?

Use the expressions in the list below in the dialogue.

take it easy	forget it
✓ cool it	have it your way

Tony: Hey, Carl. Look at those cute girls.

Carl: _Cool it_! They're looking this way.

Tony: (whistles at the girls) Hey, Baby!

Carl: ———! You're an animal, Tony.

Tony: Who are you calling an animal?

Carl: Look. They're walking away.

Tony: Let's follow them.

Carl: ———. I'm not interested.

Tony: Come on. There's nothing else to do. Walk faster.

Carl: I'm going to go home and watch TV.

Tony: ———. See you around.

17

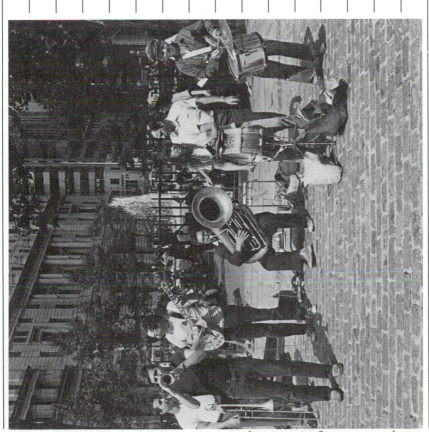

U.S. Department of Housing and Urban Development.

Before you read, answer these questions:

Are you shy when you are meeting people?
What do you ask people when you meet them?
What do you talk about?
Do people sometimes ask you difficult questions?
What do they ask you?

Say these words after your teacher or after an American friend:

hi	hon′ ey
shy	drink′ er
buy	wor′ ry
town	or′ der
close (adj.)	com′ pa ny
help	pres′ i dent
great	su′ per mar ket
fine	se′ cre ta ry
hard	co med′ i an
real′ ly	

Phrases and expressions

a lot
be good at
Really?
What do you do for a living?
the United States
ladies' room
go away

Bar vocabulary

whiskey sour
Bloody Mary
beer
scotch
on-the-rocks
Drink up.
Cheers!

As you read, think about these questions:

Who do Frank and Alan meet?
Do the women like them?
Do they like the women?
What do the men do for a living?

The two men are at the bar. They are talking to Helen and Emily.

CAN WE BUY YOU LADIES A DRINK?

Man # 1: Hello, girls. I'm Alan. My friend here is Frank.

Frank: Hi.

Alan: Come here, Frank. (*to Helen and Emily*) Frank's shy. He's still afraid of girls.

Helen: Well, I'm Helen, and this is my friend, Emily.

Frank: Can we buy you ladies a drink?

Helen: Oh . . . thank you. A whiskey sour for me.

Emily: And a Bloody Mary for me, please.

Frank: (*to the bartender*) A whiskey sour, a Bloody Mary, a beer, and a scotch-on-the-rocks. (*to Helen and Emily*) Are you girls new in town?

Helen: No, why?

Frank: We're in here a lot, and we never . . .

Alan: Here you are, girls. Drink up, there's more behind the bar!

Girls: Thank you.

Alan: Cheers! Now . . . let me see. No, don't tell me. You're a secretary.

Helen: You're close.

Alan: I'm always right. And you, Lilly . . .

Emily: Emily.

Alan: Oh, sure, Emily. You're a . . . a . . . help me, Frank.

Frank: I'm no good at guessing.

Emily: I'm a teacher.

Alan: Really? That's great.

Frank: Yeah, really great. How about another drink, honey?

Emily: No, thanks. I'm fine. Are you working here in the city?

Frank: Yes.

Emily: Where?

Frank: Here and there. Right now I'm looking for the right company. Good jobs are hard to find these days.

Helen: You're so right. I'm still working, but I'm always looking for something better.

Frank: Oh?

Helen: Yes.

Alan: Are you ready for another drink?

Helen: Not yet.

Emily: What about you? What do you do for a living?

Alan: I'm President of the United States.

Helen: No, really, Alan. Tell us.

Emily: (to Helen) Maybe he's a comedian.

Alan: I'm working in a supermarket.

Helen: How interesting!

Alan: Not really.

Frank: Emily, how about you . . . another drink?

Emily: No thanks. I'm a slow drinker.

Frank: Oh.

Emily: (to the men) Excuse us for a moment. (to Helen) Helen, please come to the ladies' room for a minute.

Helen: Yes. Let's go. (to the men) Don't go away now.

Frank: Don't worry. Can I order another drink for you now?

Cultural facts

Drinking in the United States

Do Americans drink a lot of liquor? Some do. But 33 percent of Amer-

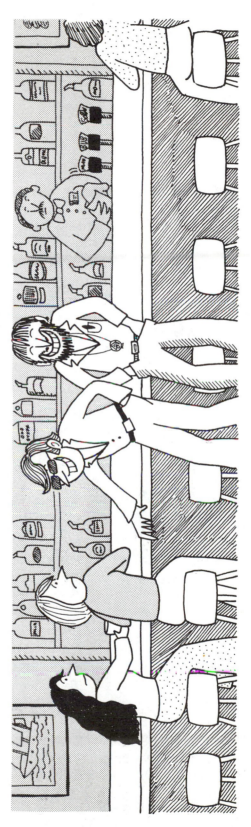

icans do not drink at all. Many Americans only drink at parties which they go to perhaps four or five times a year. Today most Americans drink water, milk, juice, soda, coffee, or tea with their meals. But wine is becoming more popular each year.

In 25 states of the United States, a person has to be twenty-one years old to buy liquor. In the other 25 states, a person has to be eighteen or older.

Is it the same in your country?

COMPREHENSION EXERCISES

Finding the Facts

If the sentence is true, write "T." If the sentence is false, write "F."

1. ___ Helen orders a beer.

2. ___ The men buy the women drinks.

3. ___ The women order a few drinks each.

4. ___ Alan is a comedian.

5. ___ Both girls go to the ladies' room.

Making Inferences

If, in your opinion, the sentence is true, write "T." If, in your opinion, the sentence is false, write "F." If you are not sure, write "M" for maybe. Discuss your answers and your reasons for them with other students.

1. ___ Frank is shy.

2. ___ Frank thinks it is great that Emily is a teacher.

3. ___ Frank doesn't have a job.

4. ___ Helen is a secretary.

5. ___ Frank is looking for a job because he isn't working now.

Written Comprehension Questions

Write the answers to the following questions:

1. Do you think good jobs are hard to find?
2. Do you think that Frank has a difficult time finding a good job? Why or why not?
3. Do you think single men go out to bars a lot?
4. Do you think Frank and Alan go out to bars a lot?
5. Why are Frank and Alan in the bar?
6. Do Frank and Alan always tell the truth. Give two examples from the story to show that they tell the truth or they do not.
7. Do you think Helen and Emily are interested in the men?

VOCABULARY EXERCISES

Select the correct words from the list below to fill in the blanks.

secretary   super
bartender   doctor
✓ *teacher*

You can usually find

1. a _teacher_ in a school.
2. a _____ in an office.
3. a _____ in a hospital.
4. a _____ in a bar.
5. a _____ in an apartment building.

Select the correct words from the list below to fill in the blanks.

new   great   hard
shy   funny   ✓ fine

1. How are you? I'm _fine_.
2. Is that your car? It's beautiful. Is it _____?
3. We're laughing because the movie on TV is _____.
4. This is a good party. Where's Judy?
   She's over there in the corner.
   Why isn't she talking to anyone?
   She's very _____.

5. I can't find the answer. The question is too _____.

6. I have a new job.
   Oh? How is it?
   It's _____. The people are nice and the salary is good.
   You're lucky.

Language Practice

Use your imagination. You're at a party. You're shy. But after a few minutes, you are tired of standing alone. There is another person standing alone. You're going over to talk to him or her.

1. Write some questions he or she is going to ask you.
2. Write your answers to the questions.
3. When you finish your dialogue, make an extra copy.
4. Give a classmate the extra copy. Practice the dialogue with him.
5. Present the dialogue to the class.

For *Grammar Practice*, see page 194.

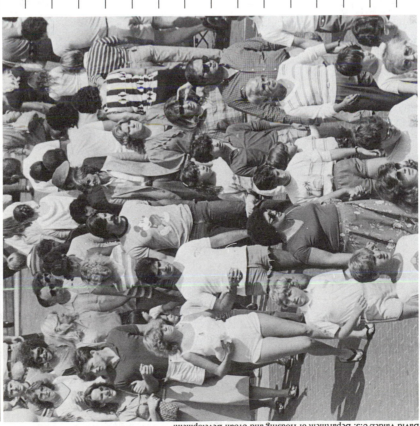

David Valdez/U.S. Department of Housing and Urban Development.

Before you read, answer these questions:

Do you like most people that you meet?

What kind of people don't you like?

What do you do when you are at a party and you meet someone that you don't like?

Is it polite to leave a party and not say good-bye to people that you met?

Say these words after your teacher or after an American friend:

jerk

straight

hope

pho′ ney

pro′ gram

id′ i ot

fan tas′ tic

Phrases and expressions

hold a conversation

turn off

in front of

waste _____ 's time

at least

As you read, think of these questions:

How do Helen and Emily feel about the men?

Which woman likes the men more?

Do they say good-bye to the men?

How do the men feel at the end of the story?

Helen and Emily are alone in the ladies' room now. Emily is angry.

WHAT ARE WE DOING HERE, HELEN?

In the ladies' room . . .

Emily: Now what are we going to do? Helen, what are we doing here? Those two guys out there are idiots. They're phonies, too. All they can do is drink. They can't even hold an intelligent conversation. Let's go.

Helen: Frank, the quiet one, is not so bad.

Emily: Come on, Helen. He's a jerk. "I'm President of the United States." I'm not going to waste another minute of my time here. At least at home I can turn off the television when I'm tired of the program.

Helen: You're right. They aren't the greatest, but it's better than sitting in front of the television.

Emily: I'm not so sure. I'm going. Are you coming?

Helen: Yes, I'm coming.

Emily: Walk straight to the door and hope they don't see you.

Helen: Aren't we going to say good-bye?

Emily: What for?

Helen: Oh Emily, that's not nice.

Emily: Maybe not, but I don't want to see them again. Now remember, walk straight to the door. Here we go.

Frank: Where are the girls?

Alan: Don't worry about it. They think we're great. They're coming back. There they are!

Frank: Look. Hey, Alan. They're leaving!

Alan: Good.

Frank: Good?

Cultural facts

Manners in the United States

Many people, including some Americans, think that Americans are rude. It is true that our manners are not as formal as the manners of many other peoples. But many Americans, like Helen, don't like to be rude.

What is polite? Lots of Americans aren't sure. But we have books to help us. In fact we have dozens of books on manners, or etiquette, to help us. We have etiquette books for men, women, and children. We have etiquette books for the office and home. We have books that tell us how to be polite in every occasion. These books may be hard for you to read, but they are there if you need them.

COMPREHENSION EXERCISES

Finding the Facts

If the sentence is true, write "T." If the sentence is false, write "F."

1. ___ Emily thinks the two men are phonies.

2. ___ The two men are intelligent.

3. ___ Helen thinks it is better to go out on a date than to sit home.

4. ___ Frank is bad.

Making Inferences

If, in your opinion, the sentence is true, write "T." If, in your opinion, the sentence is false, write "F." If you are not sure, write "M" for maybe. Discuss your answers and reasons for them with other students.

1. —— Emily isn't interested in the men.
2. —— Helen is interested in one.
3. —— Emily and Helen are interested in one.
4. —— Frank and Alan are angry when the girls leave.

Discussion Questions

Write or discuss the answers to the questions below.

1. In Emily's opinion, why are the two guys idiots?

_____

2. In Helen's opinion, what is better than sitting in front of the TV?

_____

Discussion Questions for More Advanced Students

Write or discuss the answers to the following questions:

1. Which man is more interested in the girls? Where can you find that in the story? (Find the words and write them.)
2. Which girl is more interested in the guys? Where can you find that in the story? (Find the words and write them.)

VOCABULARY EXERCISES

Select the correct word from the list below and write it in the correct blank.

> phoney   an idiot
> fantastic   straight

1. You have a new job? And a higher salary? That's _____!
2. I don't like Jerry at all. If you ask me, I think he's _____.
3. Maria is the girl that has _____ black hair.

That Alan, he's really terrible. He's not interested in Helen or me. He's only interested in women—all women. I can't _____ my _____ with him. So I'm going home.

Select an antonym for the words below.

idiot   phoney   fantastic

1. terrible _____
2. real _____
3. intelligent person _____

For *Grammar Practice*, see page 195.

4. I have a three-dollar bill.
A three-dollar bill? What are you talking about?
Here it is.
That's _____. There aren't any three-dollar bills in the United States.

Select the correct word from the list below and write it in the correct blank.

hope   waste   time
jerks

Emily: Those two guys in the bar are terrible. It's nice to get out of the house, but I don't want to spend my time with them. Well, maybe my language is too strong when I call them _____. I always _____ that I'm going to meet a nice man.

19

U.S. Department of Housing and Urban Development.

Before you read, answer these questions:

How much is a sweater today?
How much is an expensive sweater?
How much is a cheap one?
Are clothes cheaper or more expensive in your country than in the United States?
Think about the clothes that you have for a minute. What is the most expensive thing you own? A coat? A jacket? A suit? A dress?
Have you got a lot of clothes these days or only a few clothes?
Are you going to have a lot more clothes someday or isn't that important to you?

Say these words after your teacher or after an American friend:

		Phrases and expressions
dress	clo´ set	be reduced from
pink	pack´ age	be on sale
need	be sides´	be full of
clothes	af ford´	look at
wear	be lieve´	be wrong with
start	re turn´	give _____ away
sum´ mer	fa´ vor ite	can't stand _____
bar´ gain		take _____ back

As you read, think about these questions:

What does Barbara want to buy at the beginning of the story?
Why doesn't John want her to buy it?

What's wrong with her old clothes?
Why does John go out at the end of the story?

The next story is about John and Barbara and buying new clothes. They are at home in their new apartment.

MARRIED LIFE

Barbara: John, John! There's a great boutique up the street.
John: Oh?
Barbara: Yes. And there is a beautiful dress in the window. It's so perfect for me. It's pink and just right for summer.
John: How much?
Barbara: John, it's a bargain. It's reduced from $185.
John: To what?
Barbara: It's on sale. Really John, I need it.
John: But Barbara, your closet is full of clothes.
Barbara: How can you say that? I haven't got a thing to wear. Besides, it's a small closet.
John: Seriously, Barbara. Come here. Now look at all these clothes!
Barbara: Well, what about them?
John: Now look, what's wrong with this dress?
Barbara: I can't wear it.
John: Why not?
Barbara: It's too small.
John: Then give it away.
Barbara: No, I can't.
John: Why not?

Barbara: It's one of my favorite dresses.

John: All right, all right. What about this dress, and this, and this, and this?

Barbara: Well, that one's too small, and that one's too short, and that one's so old. Really, John, I'm telling you—I don't have a thing to wear, and the dress in the boutique is just perfect.

John: How much?

Barbara: Not very much, really.

John: How much? Come on, tell me.

Barbara: Only $89.

John: No, absolutely not. That's too much. That's almost 2 days' pay. NO. We can't afford it.

Barbara: John. Sit down. I have something to tell you.

John: What? Oh no, don't start crying. I can't stand it. What's

that? What's that package? No. It isn't from the boutique. Tell me it isn't from the boutique. No, I can't believe it. Barbara. What's in the package? Don't cry for heaven's sake. It's all right. Just take it back in the morning.

Barbara: I can't.

John: Why not?

Barbara: You can't return things on sale.

John: I give up. I give up.

Barbara: John? John? Where are you going?

John: Out.

Barbara: Where?

John: Out.

Barbara: When are you coming home?

John: I don't know.

Cultural facts

Buying Clothing in the United States

Americans spend about 8 percent of their income on clothing. This means that the average American family of four spends about $1,750 a year on clothing.

Is it the same in your country? Is it the same for you?

COMPREHENSION EXERCISES

Finding the Facts

Circle the correct answer.

1. There is
   a. a coat in the window of the boutique.
   b. a dress in the window of the boutique.
   c. a skirt in the window of the boutique.

2. Barbara thinks the dress is just right for
   a. a party.
   b. winter.
   c. summer.

3. The dress is
   a. on sale.
   b. not very pretty.
   c. red.

4. The price of the dress is
   a. about the same as one day of John's pay.
   b. $35.
   c. now $185.

5. At the end of the story, John
   a. is watching TV.
   b. is going out.
   c. is coming home.

Circle the correct answer.

1. The dress is
   a. still expensive.
   b. a real bargain.
   c. very bad.

2. Barbara's closet is
   a. empty.
   b. full of old clothes.
   c. full of new clothes.

3. John's pay is
   a. about $80 a day.
   b. about $74 a day.
   c. about $50 a day.

4. At the end of the story, Barbara
   a. is worried that John is angry.
   b. is happy about the dress.
   c. is angry at John.

Look at the following pictures. Study the vocabulary.

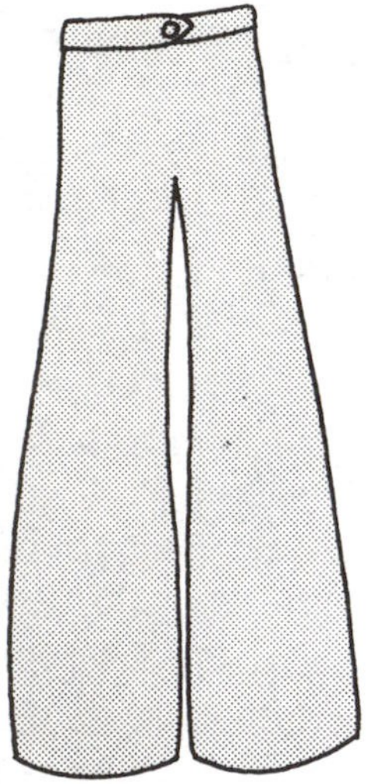

a dress shirt

slacks

a sports jacket
(or a sports coat)

a tie
(or a necktie)

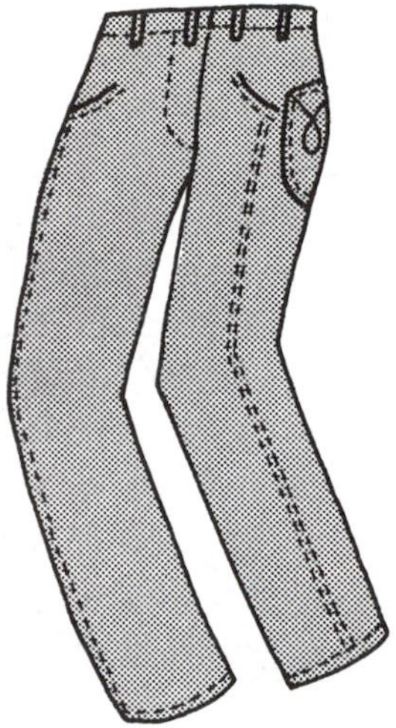

tie shoes
(or oxfords)

blue jeans
(or jeans or dungarees)

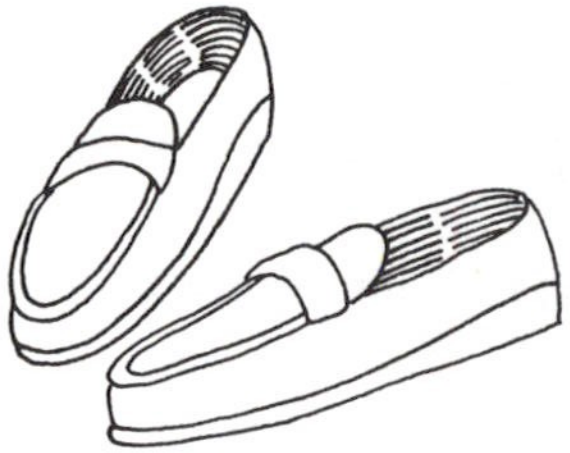

a belt

loafers

a hat

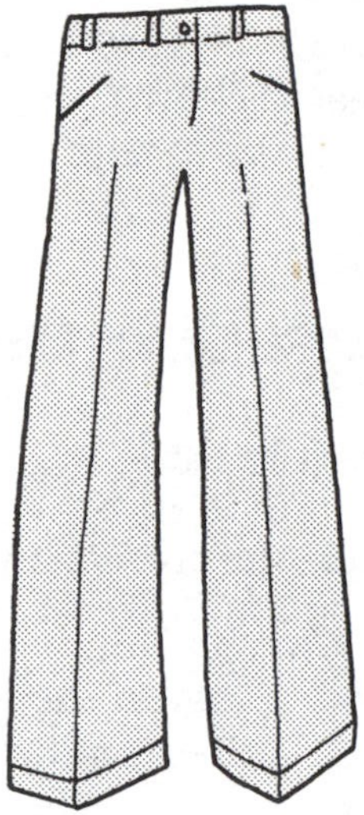

a sneaker
(or a tennis shoe)

pants

a golf shirt (or a polo shirt
or short-sleeved shirt)

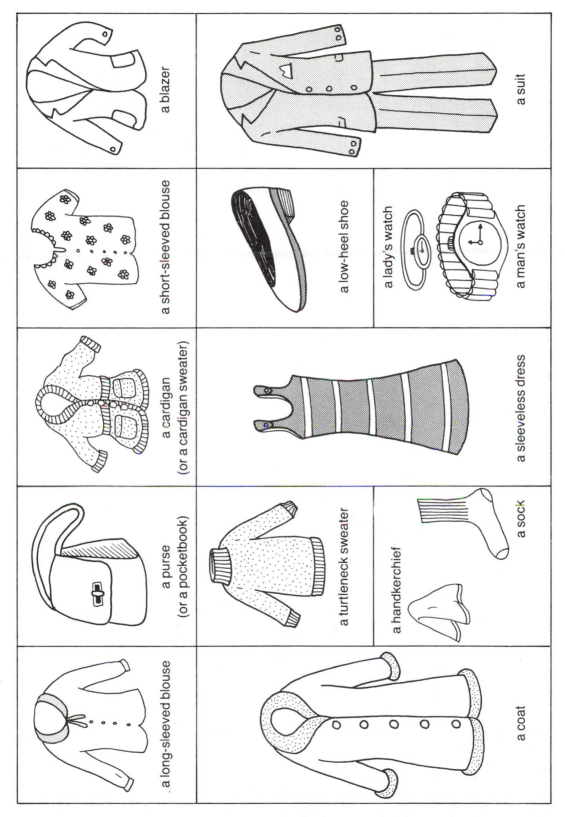

a blazer

a suit

a short-sleeved blouse

a low-heel shoe

a lady's watch

a man's watch

a cardigan
(or a cardigan sweater)

a sleeveless dress

a purse
(or a pocketbook)

a turtleneck sweater

a handkerchief

a sock

a long-sleeved blouse

a coat

Comprehension Questions

Answer the following questions:

1. Why is Barbara interested in the dress?
2. What's wrong with her other dresses?
3. How much is the pink dress?
4. Why can't Barbara return the dress?
5. Why is John going out?

Personal Exercises for More Advanced Students

1. Select one of the following topics. Tell your class about it or write about it.

a. A Time I Wanted to Buy Something Very Expensive
b. A Time I Got Very Angry in a Store and Walked Away
c. A Time I Had to Buy New Clothes

2. Discuss the following question:
What's a "happy" marriage?

3. In your opinion, what is the correct answer here? Circle it. Discuss your answer with your classmates.

a. John and Barbara are always happy in their marriage.
b. John and Barbara have got some problems, but have a normal marriage.
c. John and Barbara haven't got a happy marriage.

VOCABULARY EXERCISES

Synonyms

Select from the italicized words a synonym for each word numbered below.

pink   *take back*   *look at*

1. watch _____
2. return _____
3. light red _____

Antonyms

Select from the italicized words an antonym for each word numbered below.

winter   *start*   *like*

1. can't stand _____
2. summer _____
3. finish _____

After studying the vocabulary on the last two pages, do the following:

1. Describe yourself and what you are wearing.
2. Describe what one of your classmates is wearing, or describe what someone in your family is wearing now.

3. *Listening and conversation activity.* If you are in class now, select one student in your class. Don't look at the student too much. Describe the student. Have the other students guess who you are describing. (For example: *I'm thinking of a student. He's wearing jeans and a blue shirt. He has brown hair. His hair is long, but not too long. He is also wearing a gold ring. Who is it?*)

Exercise for More Advanced Students: Reading Newspaper Advertisements

Read the accompanying advertisement. First read these questions. Look for the answers to them when you read.

1. What's the suit reduced from?
2. What's it on sale for?
3. What's the saving?
4. What kind of suit is it?
5. What colors does it come in?
6. Can you order the suit by mail or by phone?

Now read the other two ads on the following page. Ask the other students in your class some questions about the ads. Or write some questions on a piece of paper, then give the paper to another student to answer.

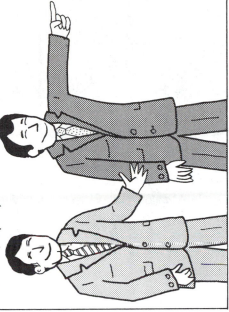

HANDSOME LIGHTWEIGHT SUITS STYLED FOR SPRING

Sale $62   Regularly $85

Fabrics you can wear now through Fall. A blend of 55% Dacron polyester, 45% wool. Two button styles with deep center vents, wide lapels. Choose now from navies, black, and browns; solid colors and stripes. Regular, short and long sizes, but not every size in every style or color. Sorry, no mail or phone orders. (Dept. 9)

Other suggestions: Buy a newspaper or use the teacher's newspaper. Find an ad that you think is interesting. Read it, then tell the rest of the class about it.

Tell the class about some clothes you want to buy. Ask them where you can go to get good quality but cheap prices. See if the class can find a sale on what you want to buy in the newspaper.

For *Grammar Practice*, see page 197.

20

U.S. Department of Housing and Urban Development.

Before you read, answer these questions:

Where were you born?

Where were your parents and grandparents born?

What dreams do you have for your life?

Are you happy in this country? If you are not, can you return to your native land?

Say these words after your teacher or after an American friend:

Spain	chil′ dren	**Phrases**
land	luck′ y	great-grandfather
dream	for′ eign	the New World
strong	coun′ try	get rich
few	per′ son	be born
past	mo′ ney	go back
house	fam′ i ly	make a home

lose	grand′ fa′ ther	native land
Cu′ ba	plan ta′ tion	after all
su′ gar	An da lu′ ci a	have no choice

As you read, think about these questions:

Where was Mr. Torres born?

Why did he come to the United States?

Can he go back to his native land?

What does he want to have someday?

How will he get these things?

The next story is about Mr. Torres. He is talking about his family and about his past. Sometimes he is happy to live in the United States; sometimes he is not.

Now read about Mr. Torres.

THE TORRES FAMILY

Our family is from Cuba. But my great-grandfather was from a small town in Andalucia in Spain. His family was very poor—no land and too many children. My great-grandfather's dream was to go to the New World and get rich.

He was lucky and strong. In a few years he was a rich man. My grandfather was rich, too. He had a large sugar plantation. My father had two plantations, so I had everything from the day I was born.

But life is strange. Here I am on 88th Street in a run-down building in a strange city in a foreign country. I know I'm never going to see my country again. But you can't go back. The past is the past.

I'm going to make a new home in this country. I'm going to have a house and a car. I'm not the first person to leave his native land. I'm not the first person to lose everything. I'm not the first person to come to this country with no money. I'm not afraid to work hard. After all, I have no choice.

Cultural facts

Immigration to the United States
Like Mr. Torres and his family, many Cubans have come to the United States. Look at this information:

Cuban Immigration to the U.S.

	1951–1960	1961–1970	1971–1979
Number of immigrants	78,900	208,500	249,700

Why do you think so many Cubans came to the United States after 1960?

Now look at the total immigration from other countries:

Immigration from 1820–1979

Country	Total Number of Immigrants
France	754,000
Germany	6,985,000
Great Britain	4,914,000
Ireland	4,724,000
Italy	5,300,000
Russia	3,376,000
Sweden	1,273,000
China	540,000
Japan	411,000
Korea	276,000
Canada	4,125,000
Cuba	539,000
Mexico	2,177,000

Which country has the most number of immigrants to the United States? Is your country on this list? How many people from your country have come to the United States?

COMPREHENSION EXERCISES

Circle the correct answer.

1. Mr. Torres was born in
   a. the United States.
   b. Cuba.
   c. Spain.

2. Mr. Torres' grandfather had
   a. a plantation.
   b. a store.
   c. two plantations.

3. His great-grandfather had a dream
   a. to have many children.
   b. to get rich.
   c. to go to the New World.
   d. both b and c.

4. Mr. Torres was
   a. a poor child.
   b. a sick child.
   c. a rich child.
   d. both a and b.

5. Now Mr. Torres is
   a. poor.
   b. rich.
   c. both a and b.

6. Mr. Torres
   a. had no money when he came to the United States.

   b. is afraid to work hard.
   c. has a house and a car.

7. Mr. Torres' great-grandfather
   a. was rich when he was in Spain.
   b. was poor when he was in Spain.
   c. was poor all his life.

8. Mr. Torres' dream is to have
   a. many children.
   b. a house and a car.
   c. a sugar plantation in the United States.

9. Mr. Torres
   a. wants to go back to Cuba, but he can't.
   b. doesn't like his native country.
   c. must stay in the United States now.
   d. both a and c.

Discussion Questions

Write your answers on another piece of paper or discuss the questions in class.

1. What was your father's dream in life? What was your mother's dream? What's your dream?

   My father's dream was to _____.
   My mother's dream was to _____.
   My dream is to _____.

2. Are you going to return to your country again? If you are, when?

3. Where were you born? Does your family still live there?

4. In the story, Mr. Torres says, "You can't go back. The past is the past." Do you agree? Why or why not?
   I agree/I don't agree because _____.

5. Read the last paragraph in the story (on page 125) again. Mr. Torres says in in the last sentence, "After all, I have no choice." What is he talking about? Is he talking about a car? Money? What?
   He's talking about _____.

6. Do *you* have a choice? Can you return to your country tomorrow?

FREE READING

People come to the United States for many different reasons. The Pilgrims and the Jews came for religious reasons. The Cubans, the Vietnamese, and the Haitians came and are still coming for political and economic reasons. Most immigrants come to the United States to find better jobs and make better lives for themselves. Millions of Irish, Italians, and Puerto Ricans came and are still coming to the United States looking for work.

Most immigrants settled in the big cities. The Irish, the Italians, the Puerto Ricans, and the Jews settled in the industrial cities of the North. And the Mexicans settled in the West. Large numbers of Cubans settled in Florida and New Jersey. Many Chinese and Vietnamese settled in California. Many Germans, Poles, and Swedes settled in the Midwest.

All of them came with a dream.

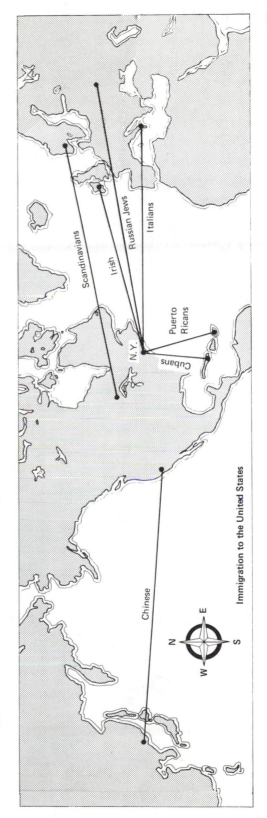

Immigration to the United States

Look at this sentence:

Many _____ left _____ for _____ reasons and settled in _____.

Use the words below to make a sentence.

Example:

    Cuba   Cubans
    political   Miami

Many _Cubans_ left _Cuba_ for _political_ reasons and settled in _Miami_.

Now make sentences with the words that follow.

1.	Jews	Russia	religious	New York
2.	Italy	economic	New York	Italians
3.	Germans	Germany	St. Louis	political
4.	Ireland	Boston	economic	Irish
5.	China	economic	San Francisco	Chinese
6.	New York	Haiti	Haitians	political

128

VOCABULARY EXERCISES

Read this information about Mary's family and notice the verbs:

1. Her mother's name is Pilar Carey.
2. Her mother's maiden name was Pilar Torres.
3. Her father's name is Joseph Carey.
4. Her grandfathers' names are Herbert Carey and Pedro Torres.
5. Her grandmothers' names are Caroline Carey and Pilar Torres.
6. Her grandmothers' maiden names were Caroline Brady and Pilar Lopez.

Look at this family tree:

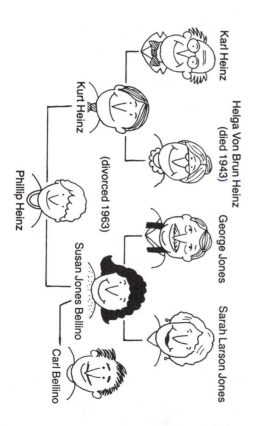

Karl Heinz

Helga Von Brun Heinz
(died 1943)

Kurt Heinz

(divorced 1963)

George Jones

Sarah Larson Jones

Susan Jones Bellino

Phillip Heinz

Carl Bellino

Read this information about Phillip's family:

1. Phillip's last name is Heinz.
2. His father's name is Kurt Heinz.
3. His mother's maiden name was Susan Jones.
4. His mother's name is now Susan Bellino because she and Phillip's father were divorced in 1963.
5. His stepfather's name is Carl Bellino.
6. His grandmothers' names are Sarah Jones and Helga Heinz. His grandmother on his father's side died in 1943.
7. His grandmothers' maiden names were Helga von Brun and Sarah Larson.

Now write about your family (as much as you know). Tell us your father's name, your grandfathers' names, and so on.

1. _____

2. _____

3. _____

4. _____

5. _____

6. _____

7. _____

8. _____

Fill in the following form:

Personal Information

Name: Mr. Mrs. Miss Ms. _____

Address: _____
        (number) (street)   *(apt. no.)*

_____
(city)   *(state)*   *(zip code)*

Maiden name
of wife _____

Name of husband _____

Children's names
(if any) _____

U.S.Citizen ( ) yes ( ) naturalized Year _____

        ( ) no If no: Student ( ) Resident ( )

            Tourist ( )

Country of Birth _____

City of Birth _____

Family

     Father's name: _____

     Mother's name: _____

     Mother's maiden name: _____

     Father's place of birth: _____
                    (city)   *(state or country)*

     Mother's place of birth: _____
                    (city)   *(state or country)*

_____
(signature)

Select a word from the list below and write it in the correct sentence.

children   lucky   houses
past   grandfather dream
strong   sugar

1. I put ——— in my coffee.

2. Many people like actors who are ——— and handsome.

3. In the ——— the Kennedy family was poor. But they have lots of money now.

4. People who have friends and a happy family are ———.

5. Cities have apartment buildings, office buildings, and factories. They don't have many private ———.

6. Some people say, "A man is rich when he has good ———."

7. I have a ———: I want to see every country in the world.

8. Carol's ——— died in 1939.

For *Grammar Practice*, see page 201.

130

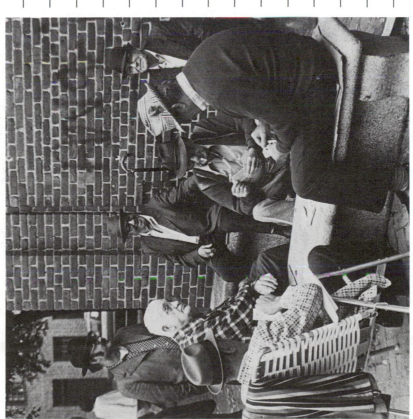

U.S. Department of Housing and Urban Development.

Before you read, answer these questions:

Did you ever buy something, but not pay for it right away?
What do people usually buy on time? Food? Furniture? Cars?
Clothes?
Is it good to buy on time?
Do you need to buy something expensive now?
How do you plan to pay for it?

Say these words after your teacher or after an American friend:

chair	hap′ pen
thief	cred′ it
spend	sales′ man
smart	com plete′
price	a like′
cost (v.)	sug gest′
down ($25 down)	fur′ ni ture
true	rea′son a ble
sound (v.)	de pos′ it
so′ fa	fa mil′ iar
arm′ chair	ex pen′ sive

Phrases
coffee table
floor lamp
savings account
the rest
a little at a time
living room set
a bunch of
buy _____ on time
finance charge
be in the same boat
Imagine that!
figure out
lots of

As you read, think about these questions:

What does Barbara want to buy?
What does John say when Barbara tells him about it?
What does Mr. Torres say about the store?
Were the prices reasonable?

In the next story Barbara wants to buy something else. Do you think she will have any problems? What will they be?

WE REALLY NEED SOME FURNITURE

Barbara: John, we really need some furniture.

John: I know. It's too bad we can't afford any.

Barbara: But we have nothing to sit on.

John: We have a few chairs.

Barbara: We have two, not a few. We need a sofa and a chair or two, and . . .

John: And?

Barbara: Yes, and a coffee table, and . . .

John: Barbara, be reasonable.

Barbara: And maybe a floor lamp. . . .

John: And who's going to pay for it? We've got only $200 in our savings account.

Barbara: The man in the store says we can give him a small deposit and pay the rest a little at a time.

John: What man? What store?

Barbara: Furniture Heaven. The store on Second Avenue. They're having a sale.

John: They're always having a sale.

Barbara: If we buy a living room set, he'll give us 50 percent off the list price. Isn't that nice? Come on. Let's go over there. I want you to see what he has.

There's a knock on the door and John opens it.

John: Mr. Torres! Come in.

Mr. Torres: Thank you, Mr. Davis. Here are your keys. They were in the door.

Barbara: Oh, they're mine. Thank you.

John: Barbara! That's the third time . . . .

Barbara: I know. I know.

John: By the way . . . Mr. Torres?

Mr. Torres: Yes?

John: You know this neighborhood.

Mr. Torres: Well, I . . . .

John: What do you know about Furniture Heaven on Second Avenue?

Mr. Torres: They're a bunch of thieves!

Barbara: No. Really?

Mr. Torres: Yes, my wife wants a new sofa for the living room.

John: Sounds familiar.

Barbara: John! Go on, Mr. Torres.

Mr. Torres: We don't have much money to spend on things like furniture.

John: We're all in the same boat.

Mr. Torres: Well, last month Furniture Heaven had a sale. They're always having sales, you know.

John: You see, Barbara?

Mr. Torres: Well, Maria saw a sofa that she liked. It was $400. But it was on sale for $299.

Barbara: Oh! That's good.

Mr. Torres: Well, she went in and told them that she wanted it, but that we would need to buy it on time. The man said, "No problem. You can have it for only $25 down."

John: Hmm.

Mr. Torres: She was so happy. She wanted to buy the sofa right away. She came home and told me about it; so I went back to the store with her to see it.

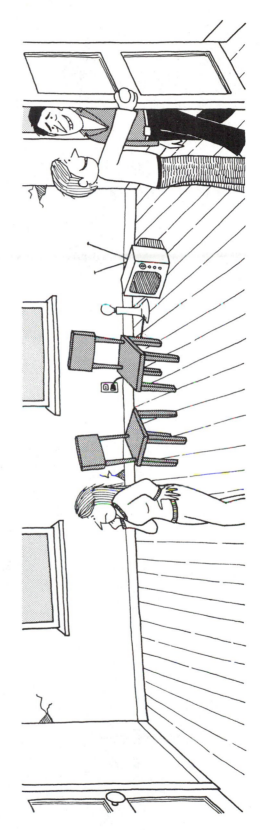

Barbara: Yes, and what happened?

Mr. Torres: The sofa wasn't anything great. But the rest was true. You could buy it for $25 down. But he didn't tell Maria about the finance charges.

Barbara: Oh?

Mr. Torres: The man said, "You have a year to pay. Only $34.25 a month."

Barbara: Well, that sounds reasonable to me.

John: Wait and see. Go on, Mr. Torres.

Mr. Torres: It doesn't take much to figure it out. $34.25 × 12 = $411 And $411 + $25 down = $436. The sofa is worth $300, maybe, but certainly not $436.

John: So the price of this great sale sofa was more than the regular price. Buying on time is expensive.

Barbara: Imagine that!

John: These salesmen are smart. They make it sound so reasonable.

Mr. Torres: They sure do. There are good sales, but you have to shop around and be careful.

Barbara: Well, we really need a sofa.

John: We'll talk about it later.

Barbara: But, John . . .

John: Later.

Cultural facts

Buying on Credit in the United States

Barbara wants to buy on credit. Millions of Americans, like Barbara, find it necessary to buy on credit each year. Very few people have enough money to pay cash for a car or a house these days. When you buy a car on time, we say you are "getting a car loan." When you buy a house or an apartment on time, we say you are "getting a mortgage."

Look at this information:

The Money Americans Owed in 1980

Home mortgages	$1,116,300,000,000
Car loans	116,800,000,000
Charge accounts	13,200,000,000

Do people buy on time in your country?

COMPREHENSION EXERCISES

Finding the Facts

If the sentence is true, write "T." If the sentence is false, write "F."

1. ___ John and Barbara have no chairs.

2. ___ At first Barbara wants to buy furniture on time.

3. ___ Mr. Torres thinks the salesmen at Furniture Heaven are honest.

4. ___ When you buy on time, you have to pay finance charges.

VOCABULARY EXERCISE

Finish the following sentences with names of furnishings (like those described on pages 136 and 137). There may be several answers possible. Write the answer you think is best.

1. Mr. Torres was tired when he got home, so he sat down in his _____ and closed his eyes.

2. The telephone rang. Mrs. Torres put her magazine on the _____ and answered it.

3. Mr. Torres' daughter, Clara, turned on the _____ because she wanted to watch a movie.

4. A friend came to see Mrs. Torres yesterday. They sat on the _____ in the living room and talked for hours.

5. After dinner, Mr. Torres wanted to read the newspaper, so he turned on the _____ next to his _____.

6. Clara likes to sit on the _____ and read because she thinks the chairs and the sofa are uncomfortable.

7. It was 6:00. It was getting dark. Mrs. Torres told

5. ____ The sale price of the sofa that Mrs. Torres liked was $299.

6. ____ Mr. Torres feels that there are good sales on furniture in the city.

7. ____ Mr. Torres thinks you should only go to one store before buying.

8. ____ Barbara decides they don't need a sofa.

Making Inferences

If, in your opinion, the sentence is true, write "T." If, in your opinion, the sentence is false, write "F." Discuss your answers and your reasons for them with other students.

1. ____ John wants to buy furniture now.

2. ____ John believes Barbara is smart about money.

3. ____ Mr. Torres and his wife bought a sofa at Furniture Heaven.

4. ____ Mr. and Mrs. Torres have a lot of money.

5. ____ John enjoys being the boss in his family.

6. ____ John and Barbara will buy furniture soon.

7. ____ John and Mr. Torres are alike in many ways.

Look at the names of these furnishings:

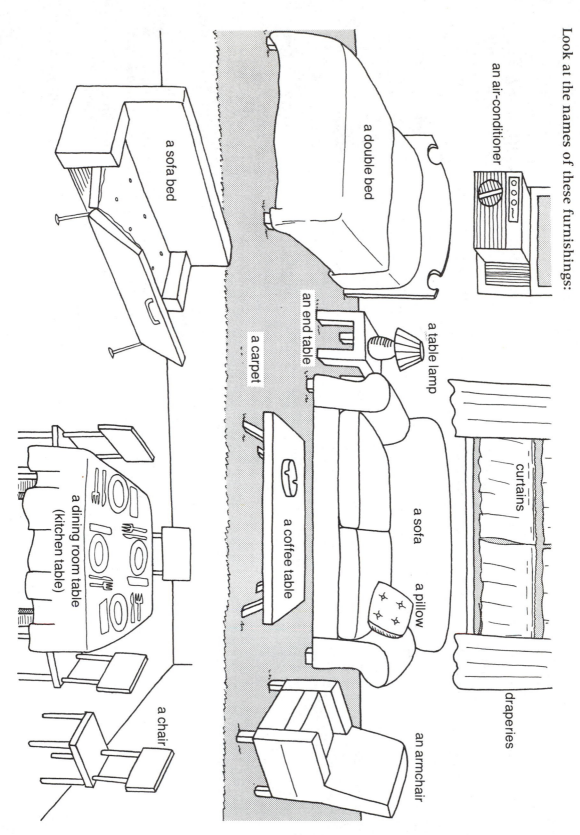

an air-conditioner

a double bed

a sofa bed

a table lamp

an end table

a carpet

curtains

draperies

a sofa

a pillow

a coffee table

a dining room table
(kitchen table)

a chair

an armchair

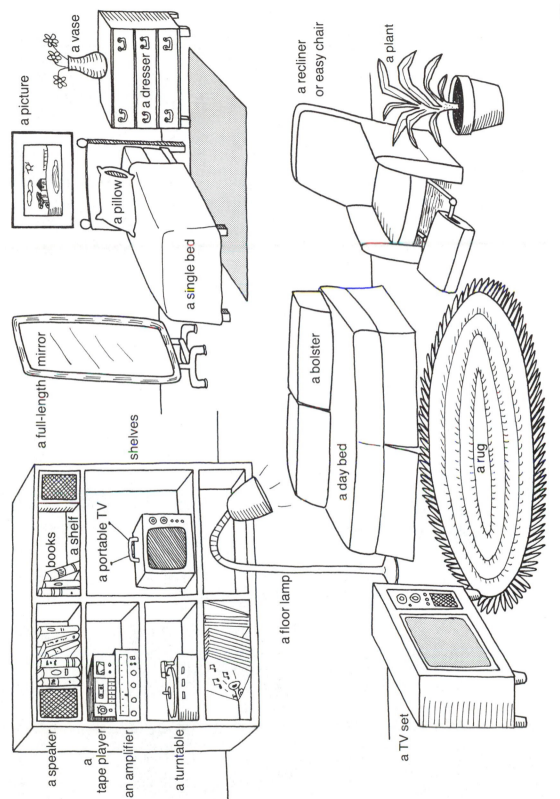

a picture

a vase

a dresser

a recliner
or easy chair

a plant

a pillow

a single bed

a full-length mirror

shelves

a bolster

a day bed

a rug

books   a shelf

a portable TV

a floor lamp

a speaker

a
tape player

an amplifier

a turntable

a TV set

137

Clara, "Close the —————. I don't want people to look in the windows at us."

8. They all sat down to eat at the —————.

9. Clara and her sister, Isabel, share one —————. They keep their sweaters, pajamas, and underwear in it.

10. Mr. and Mrs. Torres sleep in a —————.

11. Where's the dictionary? It's probably on one of the ————— in the living room.

12. The girls' bedroom is nice and large. There are two ————— for Clara and Isabel to sleep in.

13. The Torres family is quite religious. There is a ————— of Jesus Christ on the wall in their bedroom.

14. Mr. Torres wants to buy an ————— for the bedroom because sometimes it gets too hot for them to sleep comfortably.

CONVERSATION AND WRITING EXERCISES

For Beginning Students

1. Describe a room in your home. Describe the furniture.

2. Describe the same room in your home in your country. Does it look different from the room here? If so, what's the difference?

For More Advanced Students

1. One student will be the speaker. The other students take out a piece of paper. The speaker describes a room in his or her home. At the same time, the other students will draw the room. Everybody begins with the diagram on the opposite page.

> Example
>
> Speaker: There's a door. When you look in the room, on the right side next to the wall in the middle of the room, there's a sofa. There's a coffee table in front of the sofa . . .

The speaker cannot point. The other students cannot say, "Is this correct?" If they are not sure about the location of something, the students can ask questions.

> Example
>
> Speaker: There's a chair next to the sofa.
> Student: Is it on the right or on the left?
> Speaker: Wait a minute. I'll tell you. Uh, it's on the left.

When the speaker finishes, he looks at all the papers and selects those that are correct. He also explains to the other students why their pictures are not correct.

CORRECT

DOOR → COFFEE TABLE SOFA

THAT'S IT

INCORRECT

DOOR → COFFEE TABLE SOFA

NO. I SAID THE SOFA
IS NEXT TO THE WALL

2. Write a description of a perfect apartment or a perfect house. Explain what kind of furnishings it would have.

3. If your class has students from different countries, discuss what people in your country think is beautiful in a home. For example, at one time in Japan, simple rooms with very little furniture were thought to be beautiful. In France at one time, very elaborate rooms (lots of gold and decoration) were popular. What is popular today in your country? What was popular 100 years ago? Is there a difference? Compare your country to other students' countries.

FREE READING FOR MORE ADVANCED STUDENTS

The following seven stories were written by English-as-a-second-language students in New York City. Read them and then tell members of your class of an experience you had or an experience a friend of yours had in the United States or in your own country.

Last year I went to buy a stereo. When I went to this store, I saw many kinds of stereos. There was a beautiful one. It had a tape deck, a bar, and many other features. So I bought it. I gave them a deposit and asked them to deliver it to my house.

Two days later they brought the stereo, but I wasn't there when they delivered it. When I came home, I looked at the stereo and realized that it wasn't the same one I chose. I called the store immediately to discuss it. I told them, "I chose one stereo and you sent me another. I want to exchange it for the one I chose."

The man said, "I'll come and take it back tomorrow."

He didn't come.

Finally after a few days, I went to the store. They gave me some money back, so I kept the stereo they delivered.

A long time ago on the subway, a man showed me a diamond ring. I looked at it, and it looked like a real diamond. He said the price was $25. I said I didn't have that much money, and he said, "Okay. $15." I said I didn't have it, so he lowered the price again to $10. I said, "Okay," and I bought the ring.

When I got home my husband said to me, "This is not a diamond." It was a small amount of gold. That was all. I had been in New York only one month, and I didn't know this country.

Five years ago I went to an attorney to get my visa. He told me to give him $200 to start the papers, and he said I would have my visa in one year. He didn't give me any receipt. I continued to pay him every week because my visa cost $600. After a year, I was still waiting to get my visa. When I didn't get anything, I went back to his house and he told me, "I think you aren't going to get your visa." When I asked him why, he said, "Because if you don't have it by this time, it means you aren't going to get it. The only thing I can tell you is to forget your visa." I was surprised and sad, but I couldn't do anything because I didn't have any receipt. I was a tourist, and I didn't want any trouble.

After that I told the minister of the church near my house. He got a visa for me and it didn't cost me anything.

About a year ago a friend of mine was coming home from work with his brother. As they were walking, a man drove up next to them and said, "Do you want to buy a watch?" First he asked for $50, then $40, then $30.

My friend said, "I will give you $20 for the watch." Then my friend saw a watch with a gold band. My friend said, "I will give you $15 for that one with the gold band. The watch salesman said, "Okay."

Because they were trying to trick each other, they

decided to exchange the money and the watch at the same time. My friend was sitting on the man's car, so when my friend turned to get his money, the watch sales- man took the watch out of the box. After the exchange, the man took off in a hurry and went through a red light. When my friend opened the box, it was empty.

One day a magazine salesman came to the door. He sold me a few subscriptions, and I gave him a $6 deposit. He said he would come back in a few days for the rest of the money. He never returned.

A photographer came to the door and wanted to take a picture of my daughter for only $10. When the pictures were ready, the photographer wanted $49 for an album and one large photograph 8 × 10. I refused to pay what he wanted, and he refused to give me the pictures. Finally I paid $30 for them.

Five years ago a man told a lot of people that he could get visas and put the notice in the newspaper. He told each person who wanted a visa to give him $700 to begin the process. A lot of people gave him money, and when he got $20,000 he left the country. Nobody knows where he is now.

More Free Reading for More Advanced Students

In this section, you are going to read a typical *contract* that retail stores give to people who want to buy something on time.

Here is some vocabulary you should know before you begin:

Agreement: A legal paper that you must sign. It's like a contract.

I'd like to buy this sofa on time. Can I read the *agreement* first?

On credit: An amount of money that you borrow and promise to pay back.

Give me a deposit; you can pay the rest on *credit*.

Finance charge: The amount of money that you have to pay to borrow money. It's like interest.

If I sign a credit agreement to buy this sofa, how much will the *finance charge* be?

Previous balance: The amount of money you owed the store last month or the amount of money in your account last month.

Current balance: The amount of money you owe or is in your account now.

The finance charge is 1.5% each month. Your *previous balance* was $200. So your *current balance* is $203.

Previous balance	$200.00
Finance charge (1.5%)	3.00
Current balance	$203.00

Indebtedness: The total amount of money you owe. It's like your current balance.

You can pay off your total *indebtedness* anytime you wish.

Attorney: A formal name for a lawyer, a person who helps you with legal problems.

I'm not sure I want to sign this contract. I'd like to show it to my *attorney* first.

Litigation: When you go to court with an attorney to get an answer to a legal problem. It's like a trial.

If you don't pay your bill each month, the company may begin *litigation* against you.

Retail Installment Credit Agreement

This reading is an actual agreement from a store. It's typical of the kind you may find. Read this side and then the explanation if you do not understand:

1. I promise to pay the total ''unpaid balance'' as it appears on the reverse side of this agreement which includes the balance due on the purchase plus your finance charge at the monthly rates specified below in monthly installments. . . . within five days of receipt of a statement therefor.

2. I will pay a finance charge to be computed once a month on the total unpaid previous balance without deducting current payments and/or credits as of the end of each billing period as follows: 1½% per month (annual percentage rate — 18%) on the first $500 of such balance plus 1% per month (annual percentage rate — 12%) on the excess of $500, subject to a monthly minimum charge of 50¢.

Due: The time you need to pay money.

Your payment was *due* two weeks ago. You're late.

To default: To be unable to pay what you promised to pay. To break an agreement.

If you *default* on a credit agreement, you will find that you will have trouble getting credit again.

Warranty: A promise by a store or factory to repair or replace something that you bought. The warranty is usually good for a few months or years. It's like a guarantee.

If I buy this TV on sale, do I get a *warranty* with it?

This reading is an explanation of the agreement in simpler English. Read the left side, then the right side, then the left side again:

I will pay a finance charge once a month on the previous balance paying monthly installments. . . .

five days after I receive the bill each month.

I will pay a finance charge one time a month on the previous balance before I pay this month's bill.

The finance charge will be:

$0-$500   1½% per month or 18% each year

$500 + — 1% per month or 12% each year

The smallest finance charge I will pay is 50¢.

3. Upon default in payment of any installment, the entire balance shall, at your option, become immediately due and payable. I agree, further, to pay an attorney's fee amounting to 20% of the unpaid balance due and payable under this agreement should my account be referred to an attorney for collection. I may pay, at any time, the total indebtedness under this agreement.

4. To avoid delay and expense, you and I agree that any litigation hereunder shall be tried by a court without a jury.

5. In order to induce you to extend credit to me and to sell me the goods and/or services herein described, I represent that I am over the age of 21 years.

6. This is our entire agreement and cannot be changed orally. I agree that there have been no representations or warranties in connection with this sale of goods and/or services other than those which may be contained in any written guaranty or service contract duly delivered by you.

7. Where there is more than one buyer, the obligations hereunder shall be joint and several.

8. I have received an executed copy of this agreement.

NOTICE TO THE BUYER: DO NOT SIGN THIS CREDIT AGREEMENT BEFORE YOU READ IT OR IF IT CONTAINS ANY BLANK SPACE. YOU ARE ENTITLED TO A COMPLETELY FILLED IN COPY OF THIS CREDIT AGREEMENT.

This is a retail installment credit agreement, the receipt by the buyer of an executed copy of which is hereby acknowledged.

Customer's Signature:

If I don't pay an installment, I will immediately have to pay the total balance.
If I don't pay an installment, I also agree to pay for the store's lawyer. This will cost me an additional 20% of my balance.

I can pay the whole balance any time I want.

(NOTE: This is absolutely illegal. To have a trial with a jury is a constitutional right in America) You agree not to ask for a jury trial.

I am more than 21 years old.

This is the total agreement. The store did not promise me anything that the store did not put in writing. Nothing the salesman told me orally is legal.

If two people are signing the agreement, they will have equal responsibility for paying.

I have signed a copy of this agreement and have a copy of it.

DON'T SIGN THIS BEFORE YOU READ IT OR IF THERE ARE ANY EMPTY SPACES. THE SALESMAN MUST FILL IN ALL OF THE AGREEMENT NOW. ASK IF YOU DO NOT UNDERSTAND ANY PART.

This is a credit agreement and I have a copy of it.

Customer's Signature:

Here are two more agreements:

RETAIL INSTALLMENT CREDIT AGREEMENT

The details appearing on the reverse side and on any attached sale orders are a part of this agreement. They show my name and address and a descriptive listing of the goods and/or services (including the price and sales tax) which I (meaning the undersigned Buyer or Buyers) hereby purchase from you <u>Paul's Supplies</u> whose principal place of business is located at <u>143 62 St.</u>

In consideration of your extending credit to me, at your option, from time to time, I agree that all purchases of goods and/or services made by me, including mail or telephone orders, shall be evidenced by such forms as you may use and that all the provisions contained in this agreement shall apply with equal force and effect to all such purchases except that monthly terms may be increased by future agreement.

I promise to pay the total "unpaid balance" as it appears on the reverse side of this agreement which includes the balance due on this purchase and the unpaid balance, if any, on previous purchases made under my (our) account number, plus your FINANCE CHARGE at the monthly rates specified below in monthly installments within five days of receipt of a statement therefor, at the monthly terms specified on the reverse side.

I will pay a FINANCE CHARGE to be computed once a month on the total unpaid previous balance without deducting current payments and/or credits as of the end of each billing period as follows: 1½% per month (ANNUAL PERCENTAGE RATE—18%) on the first $500 of such balance plus 1% per month (ANNUAL PERCENTAGE RATE—12%) on the excess of $500, subject to a monthly minimum charge of 50¢.

If the purchase price has been increased by the addition of sales tax, I agree that any payment of a deposit or an installment includes only that proportionate part of the sales tax which is applicable to such payment.

Upon default in payment of any installment, the entire balance shall at your option, become immediately due and payable. I agree, further, to pay an attorney's fee amounting to 20% of the unpaid balance due and payable under this agreement should my account be referred to an attorney for collection. I MAY PAY, AT ANY TIME, THE TOTAL INDEBTEDNESS UNDER THIS AGREEMENT.

To avoid delay and expense, you and I agree that any litigation hereunder shall be tried by the court without a jury.

In order to induce you to extend credit to me and to sell to me the goods and/or services herein described, I represent that I am over the age of 21 years.

THIS IS OUR ENTIRE AGREEMENT and cannot be changed orally. I agree that there have been no representations or warranties in connection with this sale of goods and/or services other than those which may be contained in any written guaranty or service contract duly delivered by you.

Where there is more than one Buyer, the obligations hereunder shall be joint and several.

I have received an executed copy of this agreement.

NOTICE TO THE BUYER: DO NOT SIGN THIS CREDIT AGREEMENT BEFORE YOU READ IT OR IF IT CONTAINS ANY BLANK SPACE. YOU ARE ENTITLED TO A COMPLETELY FILLED IN COPY OF THIS CREDIT AGREEMENT.

CO-BUYER'S SIGNATURE

I understand that if the customer signing this contract fails to honor any of the terms of this contract, I may be legally required to pay the balance due.

145

Co-Buyer's Name

_____

(Signed)

Co-Buyer's Name

_____

(Printed)

Co-Buyer's
Address _____

Number   (Street)

_____

(City)   (State)

_____

(Zip)   (Apartment)

THIS IS A RETAIL INSTALLMENT CREDIT AGREEMENT, THE
RECEIPT BY THE BUYER OF AN EXECUTED COPY OF WHICH IS
HEREBY ACKNOWLEDGED

Customer's
Signature _____

SELLER:

By _____

RETAIL INSTALLMENT CREDIT AGREEMENT

In consideration of the extension of credit to me, or members of my family, by Decorations Limited, (herein called DL) from time to time for the purchase of goods and/or services (whether by mail, telephone or otherwise); I agree that each purchase shall be evidenced by such form(s) as DL may use from time to time and that DL may charge me for, and I agree to pay, the cash sales price of each item so purchased and any applicable FINANCE CHARGE, and I understand that:

1. If a bill shows a "Previous Balance," i.e., the balance owing at the start of the period covered by that bill, any FINANCE CHARGE on that bill will be based on that balance, without deducting subsequent payments or other credits or adding subsequent purchases. If a bill shows a "New Balance," i.e., the balance owing at the end of the period covered by that bill, and if I pay that balance before the end of the billing period in which DL sends me that bill, no FINANCE CHARGE will appear on the next bill thereafter sent to me on this account.

2. A minimum 50¢ FINANCE CHARGE may be imposed if the unpaid Previous Balance does not exceed $35; any greater FINANCE CHARGE will be determined by applying, as hereafter stated, a periodic rate of 1½% per month (18% corresponding ANNUAL PERCENTAGE RATE) to the first $500.00 of Previous Balance and of 1% per month (12% corresponding ANNUAL PERCENTAGE RATE) to any excess over $500.00.

3. Unless DL notifies me to the contrary, if the cash price of any purchase is paid in full within 90 days of the date of purchase, any FINANCE CHARGE thereon will be refunded or credited if requested within 30 days of full payment thereof. I will pay my account in monthly installments, based on the highest balance owing at any time, in accordance with the schedule at left (page 5).

I MAY PAY THE TOTAL INDEBTEDNESS AT ANY TIME. DL reserves the right from time to time to change the schedule (page 5) generally for all customers and upon receipt by me of notice of such change, the same shall be deemed incorporated into this agreement; provided that, in the absence of my default, DL will not arbitrarily and without reasonable cause accelerate the maturity of any part or all of the amount owing hereunder. No security interest is or will be retained or acquired under this account.

If I should default in any payment, the entire outstanding balance shall become immediately due and payable at DL's option, and, if the account is then referred to an attorney for collection, I will pay an attorney's fee not to exceed 20% of the amount then owing on the account. This agreement may be terminated at any time by either DL or myself, by notice to the other, but such termination shall not affect my then existing obligations under this agreement.

22

David Valdez/U.S. Department of Housing and Urban Development.

Before you read, answer these questions:

Are most of your friends married or single? What about your classmates?

If you are married, where did you meet your husband (wife)? Did you know each other a long time before you got married? Do you have any friends who are divorced? Why do people get divorced? Is divorce common in your country?

Say these words after your teacher or after an American friend:

		Phrases
boss	world	I mean . . .
mean (v.)	gen´ tle	
nice	wed´ ding	be married
kind	no´ tice	be over
meet	de cide´	fall in love
week	be gin´	be hurt
smile	ho´ ney moon	all of a sudden
hand	dis ap point´ ed	have lunch
whole		keep a secret
		be settled
		hold on to

As you read, think of these questions:

What does Helen tell Emily that she plans to do?
Was Mr. Beaudette married before? What happened?
Why didn't Helen tell Emily about Mr. Beaudette before?
How does Helen feel now?
Who does she call at the end of the story?

This story is about Helen. She wanted to go out and meet men. She wanted to get married more than Emily. She just came home and she's all excited.

THE ENGAGEMENT

Helen: Emily. Sit down. I have something to tell you.

Emily: Oh? What is it?

Helen: Well . . . you know Mr. Beaudette . . .

Emily: Your boss.

Helen: Yes. Well . . . we're going to get married!

Emily: What? I mean . . . uh . . . Helen, that's great. I didn't know you were seeing him.

Helen: I see him every day.

Emily: You know what I mean—*seeing him, dating him.* I thought he was married.

Helen: He *was* married. His wife left him.

Emily: When?

Helen: About a year and a half ago. He was married for fifteen years.

Emily: That's a long time. What happened, if you don't mind my asking?

Helen: I don't mind. He said that one day they decided they didn't have anything to say to each other any more.

Emily: Hmmm.

Helen: But that's all over now. He's wonderful, so kind, so nice, so good to me. He's such a loving man. I love him. I love him very much. I've never met anyone as nice as he is. He's so different from men our age.

Emily: I'm so happy for you, Helen. When's the wedding going to be?

Helen: Sometime in June. We're going to the Caribbean on our honeymoon—maybe Puerto Rico.

Emily: You've already planned the honeymoon?

Helen: Yes. And our wedding, it's going to be small—just a few friends and family.

Emily: Did you tell your mother yet?

Helen: No, not yet. She'll probably be disappointed. You know how mothers are. But I'm sure this is right. It has to be.

Emily: You're very lucky.

Helen: I know. You know, it's strange—falling in love. You notice things, little things that you never noticed before. His smile. His hands. His eyes. The city is nicer. This morning the sky was so beautiful. I don't think I ever looked up at the sky here in the city. Life is full of things I never noticed before.

Emily: Why didn't you tell me what was happening? I'm a little hurt.

Helen: At first I didn't know myself. I always thought he was very nice. Then all of a sudden we began talking, really talking. Then we began having lunch together, and . . . well, you know how it is. I wanted to tell you, but he made me promise to keep it a secret until after his divorce was final. But now everything is settled. I want to shout and tell the whole world about it!

Emily: Oh, Helen, that's beautiful. Hold on to him. I hope you'll be happy.

Helen: I will be. Don't worry about that. Oh . . . uh . . . I think I'd better call my mother now. (She calls her mother.) Hello, Mother? How are you? I'm fine, too. Mother, I have something to tell you. . . .

Cultural facts

Marriage, Divorce, and Remarriage in the United States

Many Americans marry, divorce, and remarry. Today two out of three marriages will end in divorce. Most divorced Americans will marry again. Look at this information:

	1930-1932	1951-1953	1975-1977
The number of first marriages	919,000	1,190,000	1,508,000
The number of divorces	183,000	388,000	1,070,000
The number of remarriages	138,000	370,000	646,000

Is it the same in your country?

COMPREHENSION EXERCISES

Finding the Facts

If the sentence is true, write "T." If the sentence is false, write "F."

1. ___ Mr. Beaudette is Helen's boss.

2. ___ Helen says she is in love.

3. ___ Mr. Beaudette is married.

4. ___ Mr. Beaudette left his wife.

5. ___ Mr. Beaudette and Helen are going to have a big wedding.

6. ___ Helen's mother is the first to know that Helen is getting married.

7. ___ They want to go to the Caribbean on their honeymoon.

8. ___ Helen thinks her mother will be disappointed about the engagement.

Making Inferences

If, in your opinion, the sentence is true, write "T." If, in your opinion, the sentence is false, write "F." Discuss your answers and your reasons for them with your classmates.

1. ___ Mr. Beaudette is a lot older than Helen.

2. ___ Mr. Beaudette got divorced because he was tired of his wife after fifteen years.

3. ___ Emily is happy to hear that Helen is getting married.

4. ___ Emily was hurt in an accident.

5. ___ Helen fell in love with Mr. Beaudette right away.

6. _____ Emily is sure that Helen and Mr. Beaudette will be happy together.

Stating Facts

Write or discuss the answers to the following questions:

1. Who is Mr. Beaudette?
2. How long was he married?
3. Why did Mr. Beaudette and his wife get divorced?
4. What kind of wedding do Helen and Mr. Beaudette want?
5. What does Helen think her mother's reaction will be to the news of her engagement?

Exercise for More Advanced Students: Stating Opinions

Write or discuss the answers to the following questions:

1. Why does Helen say she loves Mr. Beaudette?
2. Why do you think Helen believes that her mother will be disappointed?
3. Why didn't Helen tell Emily that she was seeing Mr. Beaudette?
4. How does Emily react to Helen's news?
   First reaction: _____
   Second reaction: _____
   Final reaction: _____

Cloze Test for Reading Comprehension

Do *not* look back at the story. Read the story below and try to write in the blanks the same word that was in the original story.

The Engagement

Helen: Emily. Sit down. I have _____ to tell you.

Emily: Oh? What _____ it?

Helen: Well . . . you know Mr. _____ . . .

Emily: Your boss.

Helen: Yes. Well . . . we're _____ to get married!

Emily: What? I _____ . . . uh . . . Helen, that's great. I didn't _____ you were seeing him.

Helen: I _____ him every day.

Emily: You know _____ I mean—*seeing* him, dating _____. I thought he was married.

Helen: _____ *was* married. His wife left _____.

Emily: When?

Helen: About a year and ——— half ago. He was married ——— fifteen years.

Emily: That's a long ———. What happened, if you don't ——— my asking?

Helen: I don't mind. ——— said that one day they ——— they didn't have anything to ——— to each other any more.

Emily: Hmmm.

Helen: ——— that's all over now. He's ——— so kind, so nice, so ——— to me. He's such a ——— man. I love him. I ——— him very much. I've never ——— one as nice as he ———. He's so ——— different from men ——— age.

Emily: I'm so happy for ———, Helen. When's the wedding going ——— be?

Helen: Sometime in June. We're ——— to the Caribbean on our honeymoon——— Puerto Rico.

Emily: You've already planned ——— honeymoon?

Helen: Yes. And our wedding, ——— going to be small—just ——— few friends and family.

Emily: Did ——— tell your mother yet?

Helen: No, ——— yet. She'll probably be disappointed. ——— know how mothers are. But ——— sure this is right. It ——— to be.

Emily: You're very lucky.

Helen: ——— know. You know, it's strange——— in love. You notice things, ——— things that you never noticed ———. His smile. His hands. His ———. The city is nicer. This ——— the sky was so beautiful. ——— don't think I ever looked ——— at the sky here in ——— city. Life is full of ——— I never noticed before.

Emily: Why _____ you tell me what was _____? I'm a little hurt.

Helen: At _____ I didn't know myself. I _____ thought he was very nice. _____ all of a sudden we _____ talking, really talking. Then we _____ having lunch together, and . . . well, _____ to tell you, know how it is. I _____ but he _____ me promise to keep it _____ secret until after his divorce _____ final. But now everything is _____. I want to shout and _____ the whole world about it!

Emily: Oh, _____, that's beautiful. Hold on to _____. I hope you'll be happy.

Helen: _____ will be. Don't worry about _____. Oh . . . uh . . . I think I'd better call _____ mother now. (*She calls her.*) Hello, Mother? How are you? _____ fine, too. Mother, I have _____ to tell you. . . .

Now that you are finished writing, look at the original story on page 148 and correct your own work. If you did not write exactly the same word—exactly the same grammar, too—then mark your answer wrong. Count the number of correct answers that you have. If you have more than 36 answers correct, then your reading comprehension is good. CONGRATULATIONS!

Free Exercise

The following exercise is a *free exercise*—do it just for fun.

Do You Want to Find an Interesting Date?

It's hard to find a good date and even harder to find a good husband or wife. Someone thought of using a computer to find a date with similar interests. Now there are computer dating-services all over the United States. Here is what the computer must know to find a date for you. Fill out the following form. Ask your teacher, another student in your class, or an American friend to explain any items or vocabulary you don't understand. After you finish, compare your answers with a friend's. Are you compatible?

1. Your age: _____ yrs. (date of birth: _____).

2. Your occupation: _____

3. Your height: _____ ft. _____ in.

4. Your weight: _____ lbs.

5. Your sex: _____ male _____ female

153

6. Your political leanings:
— middle-of-the-road — liberal — conservative
— revolutionary — none

7. Your political convictions:
— strong — average — mild — none

8. Your religion: — Buddhism — Hinduism
— Islam — Judaism — Orthodox Christianity
— Protestantism — Roman Catholicism
— (Other)

9. Your religious convictions:
— strong — average — mild — none

10. Your birthplace:
— USA — Canada — Asia — Europe — Latin
America — Africa — (Other)

11. Do you date members of other religions?
— yes — seldom — never

12. How much schooling have you completed?
— some high school — high school grad — some
college — college grad — some grad school —
advanced degree — less than high school

13. What was your favorite high school subject?
— math/science — phys. ed. — English — history — another language — art — none

14. How intelligent do you consider yourself?
— exceptionally bright — above average —
about average — below average

15. What yearly income do you consider adequate?
— $6,000 or less — $7,000 to $11,000 —
$12,000 to $19,000 — $20,000 to $29,000 —
$30,000 to $49,000 — more than $50,000

16. What languages do you speak? (mark all applicable
answers)
— English — Spanish — French — Italian
— German — Russian — Hebrew — Greek
— Chinese — Hindi — Japanese — (Other)

17. Which of the following goals is the most important
to you?
— wealth — knowledge — serenity — power
— popularity — love

18. What types of TV programs do you watch regularly?
— educational — comedies — movies — talk
— adventure — specials — serials — quiz
— westerns — variety — health — news
— musicals — drama — sport — none

19. How often do you read newspapers?
— every day — several times a week — seldom

20. What kinds of books do you like to read? (mark all
applicable answers)
— science fiction — mysteries — novels
— classics — humor — texts — nonfiction
— poetry — none

21. Which of the following activities do you enjoy?
(mark all applicable answers)
— driving — acting — bicycling — writing
— golf — card playing — studying — skiing
— playing music — thinking — drinking —
listening to music — talking — eating — fixing
things — chess — working — seeing sports
events — shopping — tennis — entertaining
— walking — partying — competing in sports

—— bowling —— gambling —— traveling —— camp-
ing —— swimming —— cooking —— resting

22. Where do you like to go when you date? (mark all applicable answers)

—— movies —— bars —— concerts and plays
—— dancing —— weekend trips —— driving around
—— dinner —— sports events —— each other's home
—— museums —— long walks —— outdoor activities

23. Which of the following words best describe you? (mark all applicable answers)

—— witty —— romantic —— conventional —— sexy
—— moody —— self-reliant —— frugal —— patient
—— optimistic —— tough —— sociable —— old-
fashioned —— tidy —— tolerant —— well-informed
—— timid —— curious —— emotional —— healthy
—— impulsive —— organized —— quiet —— capable
—— possessive

24. What sort of people are you most comfortable with? (mark all applicable answers)

—— outdoor types —— intellectuals —— artists
—— working people —— cultured —— average folks
—— professionals —— none

25. What qualities do you value most in a date? (mark all applicable answers)

—— looks —— loyalty —— intelligence —— build
—— ambition —— sense of humor —— money
—— mystery —— sophistication —— strength
—— kindness —— self-assurance —— passion
—— patience —— understanding —— virtue
—— excitement —— decisiveness —— manners

—— honesty —— punctuality —— daring —— compliance
—— sensitivity

26. What types of music do you enjoy? (mark all applicable answers)

—— classical —— folk —— rock —— country and
western —— jazz —— religious —— Latin-American
—— none

27. What is your current marital status?

—— never married —— widowed —— divorced
—— separated

28. Do you have dependent children?

—— no —— (living with me) —— yes (living
elsewhere)

29. What are your views regarding marriage?

—— the sooner the better —— not for the time being
—— would consider it with the right person —— it's
not for me

30. Do you feel that premarital sex can be justified?

—— yes —— no —— it depends

31. How often do you date?

—— almost every night —— once a week —— a few
times a week —— irregularly

32. What would your ideal future dating relationship be? (mark all applicable answers)

—— exciting —— intense —— Platonic —— sensible
—— varied —— intimate —— casual —— long-lived
—— physical —— undemanding —— exclusive
—— considerate

33. What age group do you usually date?

—— my own —— a lot younger —— somewhat

younger —— it varies —— a lot older —— somewhat
older

34. How well do you dance?
—— very well —— average —— fair —— not at all

35. How much do you drink?
—— a lot —— moderately —— little —— not at all

36. How near to you should your dates live?
—— within 15 minutes —— within 30 minutes
—— within 60 minutes —— it doesn't matter

For Grammar Practice, see page 202.

23

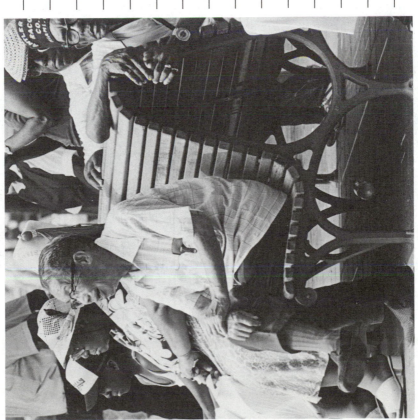

David Valdez/U.S. Department of Housing and Urban Development.

Before you read, answer these questions:

When was the last time you were sick?

Did you have a cold, a fever, the flu, a headache, or something serious?

Have you ever gone to a hospital? Were you sick or was a friend or relative sick?

Where would you feel more comfortable—in a hospital in the United States or in a hospital in your country? Why?

Tell your classmates about any experiences you have had in the United States with doctors or clinics.

Say these words after your teacher or after an American friend:

Part one		Phrases
sick	bo′ dy	mind _____'s business
care	ad′ dress	busybody
bug (v.)	ar rive′	Are you kidding?
climb	in sured′	check on
bring	ex cept′	stay with
nurse	ad mit′	give _____ a hand
sir	in′ side′	next of kin
full	out′ side′	What's the matter
mad	rel′ a tive	with _____?
near′ est	his′ to ry	medical insurance
pa′ tient	op′ er a tor	voluntary hospital
ill′ ness	vol′ un ta ry	city hospital
doc′ tor	e mer′ gen cy	I'm afraid that . . .
	i den ti fi ca′ tion	

As you read think of these questions:

Why did Bobby and Mr. Torres feel worried about Mrs. Gold?

Where did they find her?

Who did Bobby call?

What happened at the first hospital?

Where did they have to take her?

What's wrong with Mrs. Gold?

How does she feel about Bobby at the end of the story?

This story is about Mrs. Gold. As you know, she is an old woman. She hasn't been feeling well for several days. She didn't want to tell anybody or go to the doctor because she has always been proud of her good health and independence.

A FUNNY THING HAPPENED ON THE WAY TO THE HOSPITAL: PART ONE

Mr. Torres: Bobby.

Bobby: Yes?

Mr. Torres: Where's Mrs. Gold? Do you know?

Bobby: The old lady? She's at her . . . Hey, how about that? She isn't there.

Mr. Torres: I hope she isn't sick.

Bobby: She's probably inside somewhere . . . the old busybody. She has nothing to do except mind everybody's business.

Mr. Torres: That's true. And nobody cares if she lives or dies.

Bobby: Yeah. It's hard.

Mr. Torres: And you know, she likes you.
Bobby: Are you kidding? She's always bugging me. "Where are you going? Who are those friends of yours? How is your mother? Is she home?" What makes you think she likes me? She drives me crazy.
Mr. Torres: She told me.
Bobby: Oh, yeah?
Mr. Torres: Yes. You know, I think I'll check on her.
Bobby: She likes me. What? Oh, yeah, maybe we should check on her.

They go into the building. Mr. Torres knocks on her door. There is no answer. He knocks again.

Bobby: What do you think? Maybe we should call the police.
Mr. Torres: Wait. Come with me.

They go outside.

Mr. Torres: Can you climb through her window? It's open a little. I'll give you a hand.

Bobby climbs up to the window, opens it, and climbs in. He opens Mrs. Gold's door and Mr. Torres comes into the apartment.

Bobby: She's not in here, and I'm not going into the bedroom for anything.
Mr. Torres: Where's her bedroom?
Bobby: I don't know. Maybe over there.

Bobby points to a door. Mr. Torres opens it and goes in.

Mr. Torres: She's here. Call an ambulance.
Bobby: Is she dead?
Mr. Torres: No, but she looks bad.
Bobby: Operator, get me the police. Yeah, it's an emergency. Hello. We need an ambulance right away. 228 88th

Street. Apartment 1W. An old woman. We found her. I don't know. She's sick. Bobby Curtis. I live here. She isn't moving. What? How long? Fifteen minutes? Can't you send one sooner? Yeah . . . well, okay. Yes, I'll stay with her.

Twenty minutes later an ambulance arrives.

Attendant: What hospital?
Mr. Torres: I don't know. The nearest one.

They take Mrs. Gold to the nearest hospital. As they bring her into the Emergency Room, a nurse begins to question Mr. Torres.

Nurse: Who brought the patient in?
Bobby: We did.
Nurse: Your name and address, sir.
Mr. Torres: Carlos Torres. 228 88th Street.
Nurse: Are you a relative?
Mr. Torres: No, a neighbor.
Nurse: What's the patient's name?
Mr. Torres: Mrs. Gold.
Nurse: Her full name.
Mr. Torres: I don't know. I always call her Mrs. Gold.
Nurse: The patient's address?
Mr. Torres: 228 88th Street
Nurse: Who is her next of kin?
Mr. Torres: Her husband is dead. She has two married children who live out of the city.
Nurse: Can you call them?
Mr. Torres: I don't know. I don't know where they live.
Nurse: What's the matter with the patient?
Bobby: How do we know? That's why we brought her here.

Nurse: What happened to her?
Bobby: Listen. We just found her like this, all right? Do something for her.
Nurse: Does the patient have a doctor?
Bobby: Yeah, we'll take that one over there. Come on. Do something.
Mr. Torres: Bobby, you won't help Mrs. Gold by getting the nurse mad. (*to the nurse*) We don't know much about her.
Nurse: Does the patient have a history of illness?
Mr. Torres: Ma'am. I'm sorry, but we just don't know.
Bobby: She'll have nothing but history if you don't stop asking these questions. She'll be dead, lady. Where's the doctor?
Nurse: (*to Mr. Torres*) Does the patient have medical insurance?
Mr. Torres: I don't know.
Nurse: Did you bring her purse or any kind of identification?
Mr. Torres: We didn't think of it.
Nurse: You know this is a voluntary hospital, and we can't admit uninsured patients.
Bobby: What? You mean you won't take Mrs. Gold? (*to a doctor nearby*) Hey, doctor! Doctor!
Doctor: What's the problem, nurse?
Nurse: Emergency patient. No doctor, no insurance.

The doctor examines Mrs. Gold for a minute or two.

Doctor: I'm sorry, but I'm afraid we can't . . .
Bobby: I don't care what kind of hospital this is . . .
Doctor: We can't admit her here.
Bobby: Why? What do you mean you can't admit her? You have to take her. This is a hospital, isn't it?

Nurse: I'm sorry. You see . . .

Bobby: No. I don't see. And you're not sorry. You don't care. She's just another body to you.

Mr. Torres: Bobby! It's not their fault. They're only doing their job.

Bobby: Yeah, yeah. I thought doctors and nurses were supposed to help people.

Doctor: Look, son. There's a city hospital a few blocks from here. She doesn't seem to be in any danger right now.

Bobby: Seems? Seems? Don't you know?

Doctor: Look. Get her back in the ambulance fast and get moving before it's too late.

Bobby: Too late! If anything happens to this old lady, I'll never let you forget it.

Doctor: (to the ambulance driver) Municipal Hospital. And hurry!

Mr. Torres: Thank you, doctor. We didn't know.

Doctor: I'm sorry about this. Take care of your son. He's a great boy.

Mr. Torres: He's not . . . Yes, I will.

Say these words after your teacher or after an American friend:

Part two	Phrases
rest (v.)	God bless _____
try (v.)	the country
scare (v.)	lie down
breathe	May _____ rest in peace.
pain	have a heart attack
chest	treat _____ right
kiss	be worried to death

ac' cent   ask _____ a favor

diz' zy   pick a spot

PART TWO

Later that evening in the hospital . . .

Mrs. Gold: Where am I? Where am I? Help! Am I dead?

Nurse: You're in the hospital. Don't worry. You're going to be fine, just fine.

Mrs. Gold: What hospital? How did I get here? I don't remember anything. I don't want to die.

Nurse: You're at Municipal Hospital. You're not going to die. You're going to be all right. You're a lucky woman. Your neighbors found you and brought you here.

Mrs. Gold: They did? Who?

Nurse: A man with a Spanish accent and a boy about fourteen.

Mrs. Gold: God bless them.

Nurse: Rest now. Everything's going to be fine. Do you have medical insurance?

Mrs. Gold: Yes, of course.

Nurse: Then you have nothing to worry about.

Mrs. Gold: Nurse?

Nurse: Yes.

Mrs. Gold: Can I call my daughter?

Nurse: I'll call her for you. What's her number?

Mrs. Gold: I don't remember. She just moved into a new house in the country. Her husband is doing well, God bless him.

Nurse: What's her name and address?

Mrs. Gold: Mrs. Martin Green. Linda is her name. And they live in Sunnydale.

Nurse: All right. You rest now. Try to sleep.
Mrs. Gold: Did my neighbors leave?
Nurse: Yes. Good night. Call me if you need anything. I'll be right down the hall.

The nurse leaves the room. A few minutes pass and then Mrs. Gold hears a noise.

A voice: Psssst. Mrs. Gold! Where are you? Mrs. Gold?
Mrs. Gold: What? Who is it?
Bobby: It's me, Bobby. Are you sleeping?
Mrs. Gold: Bobby, what are you doing here? Come in before the nurses see you.
Bobby: They don't scare me.
Mrs. Gold: Bobby, you're terrible.
Bobby: Yeah.
Mrs. Gold: Bobby, thank you.
Bobby: What for?
Mrs. Gold: How did you find me? You know, I don't remember a thing. What time is it?
Bobby: I guess it's around 10:00 P.M. now.
Mrs. Gold: This afternoon, after lunch . . . I didn't feel so good, so I opened the window to get some air. I couldn't breathe, and I got so dizzy. So I decided to lie down. I got up from my chair at the window, you know, where I always sit, and then I felt such a pain in my chest . . . . After that I don't remember anything. Do you remember my husband, may he rest in peace.
Bobby: No.
Mrs. Gold: He had a heart attack, and now that I think of it, I felt the same way . . . . And I'm still here.

Bobby: Yeah. Hey, what's the matter? Don't cry, Mrs. Gold.
Mrs. Gold: Let an old lady cry, Bobby.
Bobby: I didn't mean it when I called you an old lady.
Mrs. Gold: But I guess it's true now.
Bobby: I'm sorry. Well, I just came to see if they were treating you all right. You let me know if they aren't. I'll take care of them.
Mrs. Gold: Yes. You're a good boy. Bobby, your mother is probably worried to death about you. Did you call her?
Bobby: I'd better be going home.
Mrs. Gold: Oh, before you go, I want to ask you a favor.
Bobby: Sure. What is it?
Mrs. Gold: Let an old lady give you a little kiss.
Bobby: Sure. Why not? All the girls love me. Just pick a clean spot.
Mrs. Gold: Oh, Bobby, you're terrible!

Cultural facts

Cost of Medical Care in the United States

Health care in America is very expensive. Look at this information.

Amount Spent for Medical Care in One Year	
1950	$ 12,700,000,000
1960	$ 26,900,000,000
1970	$ 74,700,000,000
1980	$249,000,000,000

Is health care getting more expensive in your country, too?

The Average Cost of Medical Treatment per Person

1950	$ 82.00
1960	$ 146.00
1970	$ 358.00
1980	$1,075.00

The average hospital bill for a major illness (heart attack, serious accident, cancer) is almost $50,000.
Is it good that Mrs. Gold has insurance?

COMPREHENSION EXERCISES

Finding the Facts

If the sentence is true, write "T." If the sentence is false, write "F."

1. ___ Bobby climbed into Mrs. Gold's window to get into her apartment.

2. ___ Mrs. Gold looked good when they found her.

3. ___ Bobby called the hospital for an ambulance.

4. ___ The first hospital did not accept Mrs. Gold as a patient because she did not have any money with her.

5. ___ Mrs. Gold's husband died of cancer.

Making Inferences

If, in your opinion, the sentence is true, write "T." If, in your opinion, the sentence is false, write "F." Discuss your answers and your reasons for them with your classmates.

1. ___ Bobby does not want to go into Mrs. Gold's bedroom because he's afraid she is dead.

2. ___ Mrs. Gold likes to cry.

3. ___ Mrs. Gold likes Bobby very much.

4. ___ Nobody cares if Mrs. Gold lives or dies.

5. ___ A private hospital (voluntary hospital) must accept all patients.

6. ___ A public hospital must accept all patients.

7. ___ The doctor in the voluntary hospital does not care about patients at all.

8. ___ Mrs. Gold was not really sick.

Discussion Questions for More Advanced Students

1. What happened to Mrs. Gold? Describe her illness and what happened to her.

2. Why didn't the first hospital accept Mrs. Gold?

3. Why did Bobby go to Mrs. Gold's hospital room to check on her?

4. Will the hospital near your house or near your school take emergency patients if they do not have medical insurance? Find out!

VOCABULARY EXERCISES

Synonyms

Select the italicized word or phrase that means the same or about the same thing as the definitions below.

hospital ✓operator next of kin
busybody patient nurse

1. A person who makes and answers telephone calls: _operator_

2. A place to go when you are seriously sick: _____

3. A person who is interested in other people's business: _____

4. A person who is sick in a hospital: _____

5. A person who takes care of sick people: _____

6. The person who is your closest living relative: _____

Fill in the Blanks

From the list of phrases, fill in the blanks.

What's the matter with . . . ?
Are you kidding?
the country
medical insurance
give_____ a hand
worried to death

1. I hope he does not get seriously ill. He does not have any _____.

2. _____ Harry? He looks sick.

3. _____ me _____. Help me move this table. It's heavy.

4. _____ I would not try to climb that mountain. It's too dangerous.

5. I'd like to live in _____. I like the clean air and the quiet.

6. It's 3:00 A.M. I'm _____. Bobby was supposed to be home six hours ago.

24

DEUTSCH-AMERIKANISCHER BÜRGERVIERE
PRESENTS
THE GERMAN FESTIVAL

David Valdez/U.S. Department of Housing and Urban Development.

Before you read, answer these questions:

What do people in your country like to do on weekends?
What do they do on the weekends in the summer?
Have you ever gone to the beach?
What was the best time you ever had on an all-day trip?

Say these words after your teacher or after an American friend:

			Phrases
beach	rub (v.)		find out
wait	car' ry		out loud
park (v.)	bor' row		tuna fish
swim	li' cense		bathing suit
race (v.)	sand' wich		dry off
splash	hand' some		run away
freeze	tow' el		take ____ away
food	shoul' der		know ____ 's way
sand	fin' ish		around
fast	shi' ver		
make (construct)	with' out		
far	ser' i ous		
hear (v.)	Sat' ur day		
wish (v.)			

As you read think about these questions:

Where does Bobby take Isabel?
What does Isabel make for Bobby?
What does Bobby do when they get to the beach?
Do they have a good time?
Why does Bobby feel funny at the end of the story?

The next story is about Bobby and Isabel. Bobby has been watching Isabel grow up for about a year. But he has been afraid to ask her for a date because Mr. Torres is a very strict father. He decides that he has waited long enough. Read the story to find out what happens.

A DAY AT THE BEACH

Isabel: Thanks for walking me home from school.
Bobby: Sure. Uh, so what are you doing tomorrow?
Isabel: I always help my mother clean on Saturday.
Bobby: It's going to be too hot to clean tomorrow. Why don't you come to the beach with me?
Isabel: My father won't let me.
Bobby: How do you know? Ask him.
Isabel: I don't know. . . .
Bobby: Come on. You're not a kid anymore. Ask him. Here he comes. Do it.

Isabel: Hi, Dad. Daddy?
Mr. Torres: Hello, sweetheart. Bobby.
Isabel: Daddy, can I go to the beach tomorrow . . . with Bobby?
Mr. Torres: Well . . .
Isabel: Please?
Mr. Torres: I . . . uh . . .
Bobby: Gee, thanks, Mr. Torres.
Mr. Torres: Not so fast, Bobby.
Bobby: What? I'll take care of her.
Isabel: Please, Dad? Please?
Mr. Torres: Well . . . all right. But be careful and be home before dark.

Bobby: Thanks, Mr. Torres.
Isabel: Thanks, Dad.
Mr. Torres: Come upstairs now and help your mother with dinner.
Isabel: (to Bobby) What time?
Bobby: Early. Nine o'clock. Then we can have the whole day.
Isabel: Okay. See you tomorrow at 9:00.

The next day Isabel meets Bobby in front of the building.

Isabel: My father really likes you.
Bobby: Oh yeah?
Isabel: He said you were a fine young man.
Bobby: Yeah? Your old man is okay. What are you carrying there?
Isabel: I made lunch for us.
Bobby: No kidding. Did you make it yourself?
Isabel: Yes.
Bobby: What did you make?

Isabel: I'm not going to tell you. Wait and see.
Bobby: Tell me.
Isabel: No.
Bobby: Girls!
Isabel: What about them?
Bobby: I love them. Hey, look, let me carry that.
Isabel: Thank you. It's heavy.
Bobby: Nah, it's light. Come on. This way.
Isabel: Why are we walking this way?
Bobby: The car is parked on the corner.
Isabel: The car? What car? You don't have a car.
Bobby: I borrowed one.
Isabel: But you don't have a license, do you?
Bobby: I borrowed a license, too.
Isabel: What? You can't do that. What if my father found out?
Bobby: He won't find out.
Isabel: We can't. I'm afraid.

Bobby: Don't worry. I won't let anything happen to you. Come on. Get in.

Two hours later they arrive at the beach.

Isabel: This is a beautiful beach, Bobby. How did you find it? I didn't know there were any beaches like this so close to the city. There's hardly anyone here.
Bobby: You've got to know your way around.
Isabel: I guess so. Let's go swimming.
Bobby: I'll race you.

They run to the water. Isabel puts her feet in the water and stops.

Isabel: It's freezing. Bobby, don't! Don't splash me! Stop—please. PLEASE!
Bobby: It's warm. Come on. Come on in. I'll race you to that rock out there.
Isabel: No, it's too far. Come back.
Bobby: Okay. Stay there. I'm going to swim out to the rock.
Isabel: (*to herself*) He's crazy—driving without a license, swimming out there alone.

She watches him swimming.

He swims well. He's strong. He's crazy, but he's nice, too. He has such a nice smile.

She watches him for a moment and then calls to him.

Bobby! Come back!

She turns and walks up the beach and thinks to herself.

He can't hear me. Well, I guess he knows what he's doing. He can take care of himself. Worry won't do any good anyway.

I think I'll get the food ready. I hope he likes tuna fish sandwiches.

She takes the food out of the picnic basket and arranges it on the blanket.

Bobby: BOO!
Isabel: OH! Oh, Bobby, you scared me!
Bobby: It's okay.
Isabel: You really scared me.
Bobby: I'm sorry. I didn't mean to—really I didn't.
Isabel: Well, I'm glad you're here. I was worried about you out there.
Bobby: You were? You don't have to worry. I can take care of myself.
Isabel: I know you can, but still I was worried. Oh, look, you're shivering.
Bobby: I'm okay.
Isabel: Here. Take the towel.
Bobby: Thanks. Hey, when do we eat? I'm hungry.
Isabel: Right now. Do you want a sandwich?
Bobby: Sure.
Isabel: You're still shivering. Give me that towel.

She takes the towel, puts it around his shoulders, and begins to rub his back.

Bobby: Mmmmmm. You . . . uh . . . make great sandwiches.
Isabel: Really? I'm glad you like them. Have another.
Bobby: Let me finish this one. Here's the towel. I'll dry off in the sun. This is the life . . . a beautiful day, a nice beach, a great lunch, and a pretty girl. Let's run away and see every beach in the world.

Isabel: Don't be silly.
Bobby: Come on. It sounds great, doesn't it? And besides, I have nothing to go home to.
Isabel: Don't talk like that.
Bobby: But . . . .
Isabel: But what?
Bobby: Nothing.
Isabel: Tell me.
Bobby: I wish I could be happy like this all the time.
Isabel: Well, nobody can take this day away from us.
Bobby: Yes, but . . . .
Isabel: No "buts." Don't talk. Smile. You know, you have a nice smile. Why don't you smile more often?
Bobby: I'm not usually this happy.
Isabel: Why?
Bobby: You ask too many questions.
Isabel: Mmmm. You know, your hair is the same color as the sand.

She touches his hair.

Bobby: Don't.
Isabel: What?
Bobby: Don't. I feel funny.
Isabel: Maybe it's the tuna fish sandwiches.
Bobby: Be serious.
Isabel: Okay. I'm sorry.
Bobby: I'm sorry, too. You know, sometimes I wish . . .
Isabel: Me, too.

Cultural facts

Dating in the United States

Most American young people begin to date when they are twelve years old. At first, boys and girls go out together in groups or are supervised at school or church dances. By the time they are fifteen, most American teenagers go out on dates alone. However, most parents tell their teenagers when to be home—10:00 P.M. for young teens and midnight for older teens. Most parents do not allow their teenagers to date on school nights. They can only date on the weekends.

Is it the same in your country?

COMPREHENSION EXERCISES

Finding the Facts

If the sentence is true, write "T." If the sentence is false, write "F."

1. ____ Isabel believes that her father likes Bobby.

2. ____ Isabel's mother made lunch for Bobby and Isabel.

3. ____ Bobby has a driver's license.

4. ____ Isabel goes swimming.

5. ____ Bobby feels funny because he isn't enjoying his day with Isabel.

6. ____ Bobby has black hair.

Making Inferences

If, in your opinion, the sentence is true, write "T." If, in your opinion, the sentence is false, write "F." Discuss your answers with your classmates.

1. ___ Mr. Torres is a strict father.

2. ___ Bobby is surprised to learn that Mr. Torres likes him.

3. ___ Bobby likes to show Isabel how strong he is.

4. ___ Bobby isn't happy with his life.

5. ___ Bobby feels funny because of the tuna fish sandwiches.

Exercises for More Advanced Students: Stating Opinions

Finish the following sentences by using information from the story on page 166 and by giving your opinions. Discuss your answers with your classmates. It is possible that there are many different answers that are correct or possible for each sentence?

1. Bobby asked Isabel to go to the beach because

_____

2. Mr. Torres gave Isabel permission to go to the beach with Bobby because _____

3. Isabel was afraid to ride in the car with Bobby because _____

4. Bobby says that he has nothing to go home to because _____

5. Bobby and Isabel at the end of the story wish they _____

Predicting Outcomes

Answer these questions using information that you know about the people in the story.

1. What do you think will happen with Bobby and Isabel? Will they continue to see each other?

2. Do you think Mr. Torres will find out about Bobby's driving without a license?

3. Do you think Isabel will tell her parents everything that happened on her date with Bobby? What will she tell them?

4. Will Bobby get Isabel home before dark?

Speculating About Past Events

Answer the following question using information from the story and your knowledge of the world.

1. Several bad things could have happened to Bobby and Isabel during the story. They didn't happen, but they could have happened. List several things that could have gone wrong.

VOCABULARY EXERCISE

From the list of words that follows, select the word that best completes each sentence.

    carried   *borrowed*   *shivered*
    license   *sandwich*   *beach*

1. I wanted to go swimming, so I went to the
    _____.

2. You need a _____ to drive a car.

3. I like to eat a _____ for lunch.

4. It was so cold. I sat on the beach and _____.

5. The man got out of the taxi and _____ his suitcases into the hotel.

6. I didn't have a car then. So, when I really needed one, I _____ a friend's car.

25

U.S. Department of Housing and Urban Development.

even (adv.)   wonder (v.)   join the parade
gift   senior citizen center
                              son-in-law

As you read, think of these questions:

How is Mrs. Gold doing these days?
Who is Michael?
Who is Bobby married to?
Why are they giving a party for Bobby?
Has Bobby changed?

It is ten years since Bobby took Mrs. Gold to the hospital. Bobby and Isabel are walking down 88th Street toward the building where they lived. They are talking about the street. Read the story and find out what has happened to Bobby, Isabel, and Mrs. Gold.

A VISIT

Bobby: It still looks the same.
Isabel: The same old buildings, the same noise.
Bobby: The same double-parked cars.
Isabel: Look, there's Mrs. Gold. There she is in the window. It's good to see that some things don't change. She's looking well, isn't she?
Bobby: An amazing old lady. She must be about seventy-five now. I wonder if she'll recognize us.

Before you read, answer these questions:

Many things have happened in your life in the last few years. If you saw an old friend and your friend asked you, "What have you been doing since I saw you last?" what would you say?
Do you know anyone who has had a baby lately? Anyone who has gotten married? Anyone who has gotten a promotion? Who were they?
Do you have any special plans for your future? What are they?

Say these words after your teacher or after an American friend:

As this is the last chapter of the book, we would like you to look up this chapter's words in an English dictionary (not a translation dictionary). Find out how they are divided and where the primary accent is.

For example, if you look up the word *amazing* on the list below, you may find something like this: amaze \ ə-māz\ v. amazed; amazing. From this information you can see that *amaze* has two syllables (\ ə-māz\) and that the stress is on the second syllable (\ ə-māz´\). You can see that *-ing* is a third syllable (a maz ing). So, you can put all this information together and write: a maz´ ing.
Now do the *words* (not the phrases) that follow.

Words		Phrases
amazing	manager	double-parked
big	night	go by
change (v.)	occasion	get out of
charmer	recognize	go on
celebrate (v.)	realize	look like
	promotion	

Mrs. Gold: Bobby! Is that you? And Isabel! It *is* you. It's wonderful to see you again. And, look! Who's this?

Bobby: Say "hello," Michael.

Michael: Hello.

Mrs. Gold: Michael—that's a nice name. And how old are you?

Isabel: He's three and a half, aren't you?

Michael: Three and a half.

Mrs. Gold: Such a big boy. He looks just like Bobby.

Isabel: Everybody says that.

Bobby: Handsome like his father, right Isabel?

Mrs. Gold: Bobby, you haven't changed a bit.

Bobby: You haven't, either. You're looking good.

Mrs. Gold: Don't lie to me, young man. I look older every day.

Bobby: Older, but prettier—just like old gold.

Mrs. Gold: Such a charmer you married, Isabel.

Isabel: I know.

Mrs. Gold: I think your family is waiting for you upstairs, Isabel, why don't you go up with little Michael. And Bobby, make an old lady happy . . . stay and talk to me for a few minutes.

Bobby: Sure. Tell them I'll be up in a little while.

Isabel takes Michael upstairs and Bobby goes into Mrs. Gold's apartment. He sits down and they begin to talk.

Mrs. Gold: So tell me.

Bobby: What?

Mrs. Gold: "What?" He asks me, "What?" Tell me what has been happening with you.

Bobby: Well . . .

Mrs. Gold: Your mother tells me that you bought a house in Carlton.

Bobby: Yes. It's not much—a little place, but we like it.

Mrs. Gold: Not much! I'm sure it's beautiful.
Bobby: It's a start. But, tell me about yourself. How are you?
Mrs. Gold: How should an old lady be? Pains here, pains there. . . .
Bobby: Oh, sorry.
Mrs. Gold: And the landlord still takes the rent and the super is never around when you need him and there are these young boys in the neighborhood. . . .
Bobby: Mrs. Gold! (Bobby laughs.) And how is your family?
Mrs. Gold: I don't see them as much as I would like to, but they're fine, just fine. Anyway . . . um . . . Bobby, do you remember the night you took me to the hospital?
Bobby: How could I forget?
Mrs. Gold: About ten years ago, wasn't it?
Bobby: Was it that long ago?
Mrs. Gold: Yes. Well, a lot as changed since then. I used to feel very sorry for myself, but I don't anymore. When I got out of the hospital, I realized that every day was a gift at my age. I don't sit at the window all day anymore. I go out to the senior citizen center and see friends. And, I even go to school at night. You know, the world is full of interesting people and interesting things to do. When I came out of the hospital, I decided right then and there to get out and join the parade—not sit and watch it go by from my window.

Bobby: Good for you! You're a grand old lady.
Mrs. Gold: How you talk! Come and help me up the stairs.
Bobby: Oh, you're coming up, too? What's going on?
Mrs. Gold: Don't ask questions, young man. Help me up.

They go upstairs to the Torres' apartment. They knock on the door and Mrs. Curtis opens it.

Bobby: Mom! Hey, what's going on here?
Mrs. Curtis: Come in, Bobby, Mrs. Gold. We're having a party.
Bobby: What's the occasion?
Mr. Torres: Bobby, we wanted to celebrate your promotion.
Bobby: Isabel! You've been talking again.
Isabel: Why not? We're proud of you.
Mrs. Curtis: Tel us about it, Bobby. Isabel wouldn't because she wanted you to have the fun of telling us.
Bobby: There's nothing much to say. They made me the sales manager.
Mrs. Gold: Imagine, Bobby a manager! Wonderful!
Isabel: He's the best salesman they've ever had.
Mrs. Gold: The best! Imagine!
Mr. Torres: We're all very proud of you, Bobby. One day you'll be the president of the store. I'm sure of it.
Bobby: Well, I don't know, but I hope so. Then Isabel and I will buy a house on the beach. We love the beach, don't we, honey?
Mrs. Gold: He sounds just like my son-in-law, God bless him.
Bobby: Yeah, but who's handsomer—your son-in-law or me? Me, right?
Mrs. Gold: Oh, Bobby, you'll never change!

Cultural facts

Planning for a Family in the United States

Most Americans expect to marry, have children, buy a house, and live to be seventy years old or more.
Is it the same in your country?

COMPREHENSION EXERCISES

Finding the Facts

Circle the best answer by using information from the story.

1. In Bobby's opinion, 228 88th Street has
   a. changed.
   b. has not changed.
   c. has changed a little.

2. Bobby and Isabel have bought
   a. a house.
   b. an apartment.
   c. a house on the beach.

3. Bobby thinks Mrs. Gold looks
   a. terrible.
   b. old.
   c. good.

4. In his new job, Bobby will be
   a. a salesman.
   b. the sales manager.
   c. the store president.

5. Bobby says that someday he wants to live
   a. in the city again.
   b. in his own house.
   c. in a house on the beach.

Making Inferences

Circle the best answers.

1. Mrs. Gold
   a. is living the same way she used to.
   b. goes out more than she used to.
   c. stays home more than she used to.

2. Michael is
   a. Bobby's son.
   b. Isabel's son.
   c. Bobby and Isabel's son.

3. Bobby
   a. told his mother that he got a promotion.
   b. didn't tell his mother that he got a promotion.
   c. doesn't want his mother to know that he got a promotion.

Stating Facts

Discuss these questions with your classmates and then write down the answers.

1. How has Bobby changed since he lived on 88th Street? Give two examples.

2. How has Mrs. Gold changed since her heart attack? Give two examples.

3. How have Bobby and Mrs. Gold *not* changed? Give examples.

Stating Opinions

1. What do you think of the way that older people live in the United States?
2. Do you think that most Americans (like Bobby) can live better lives and have more money than their parents?
3. What do you think of American families? Are they close enough? Do they see each other enough? Do they love each other enough?
4. What do you think of life in the United States?

VOCABULARY EXERCISE

From the list below, select the words that best complete the sentences.

  amazing   charmer   celebrate
  gifts   occasion   promotion
  recognize   realize   goes by
  looks like   going on

1. Time _____ so quickly. One day you're a teenager, the next day you're forty years old.
2. This man I know is _____. He can hear a person's name only once and remember it for years.
3. I'd like to get a _____. I could use more money and I'd like more interesting work.
4. What's _____ in your life these days? I haven't seen you for months.
5. Watch out for that guy if you do business with him. He's a real _____, but he's not very honest.
6. Some people believe that a strong mind and a healthy body are _____ from God.
7. Why are you having a party? What's the _____?
8. Oh! I have to go home. I didn't _____ that it was so late.
9. Well, to tell you the truth, when I saw Harry he had changed so much that I didn't _____ him.
10. You won $1,000? Well, let's go out and _____!
11. The older Michael gets the more he _____ his father.

WRITE YOUR OWN BOOK

The last chapter of *No Hot Water Tonight* does not tell us what happened to Emily, Helen, John, and Barbara. Either alone or with your classmates, decide on *one* character (Emily, Helen, John, or Barbara) that you thought was interesting. Write a final chapter for that character. Write what you think happened to that person.

After you finish, give your chapter to your teacher. Your teacher will reproduce the stories so everyone in class can read them. We would like to read them, too, if you would like to send them to:

Jean Bodman and Michael Lanzano
c/o The English Editor, College Division
Macmillan Publishing Company
866 Third Avenue
New York, New York 10022

Supplementary Exercises

CHAPTER 1

Verb Practice

Circle the correct form of the verb.

Hello. My name (am (is) are) Mrs. Gold. Here I (am is are) every day—here at my window. In the morning, in the afternoon, and in the evening I (am is are) here—alone. My husband (am is are) dead, and my daughter and son (am is are) married. I (am is are) still here in this old building.

The people in this building (am is are) interesting. They (am is are) different. Some (am is are) from Europe. Some (am is are) from Latin America. Some (am is are) married, and some (am is are) single. Married, single, young, or old, we (am is are) neighbors. Their life (am is are) my life now.

CHAPTER 2

Question Practice

Look at the words and make questions.

Example:
How you are ?

How are you ?

1. Where mother your is ?

   _____

2. Who boys those are ?

   _____

3. How they old are ?

   _____

Verb Practice

Read the original story again (page 8). In the correct exercise, select the correct form of the verb. Circle the correct form. Do not look at the original story when you write.

Mrs. Gold: Bobby! Hello, Bobby!

Bobby: What?

Mrs. Gold: How (am is (are)) you, Bobby?

Bobby: Okay.

Mrs. Gold: Where (*am is are*) your mother? (*Am Is Are*) she at home?

Bobby: No. She (*am is are*) at work. She (*am is are*) never home.

Mrs. Gold: I (*am is are*) sure she (*am is are*) very busy.

Bobby: Sure. Sure.

Mrs. Gold: Who (*am is are*) those boys?

Bobby: They (*am is are*) my friends. Why?

Mrs. Gold: How old (*am is are*) they?

Bobby: Eighteen or nineteen, Why?

Mrs. Gold: But Bobby, you (*am is are*) only fourteen.

Bobby: Yes, and you (*am is are*) an old lady.

Mrs. Gold: Bobby!

CHAPTER 3

Verb Practice

Write the correct form of the verb in the empty spaces. Use *am*, *is*, or *are*. Do *not* look at the original story. Use contractions (*'m, 's, 're*).

That 'e Bobby Curtis. Angry? No, I 'm not

angry. Bobby ___ a problem. I feel sorry for him. And his mother, I feel sorry for her, too. She ___ at work all day. Bobby ___ usually in school, but today he ___ with those boys. Who ___ those boys? They ___ new in this neighborhood. Where ___ they from?

I ___ worried.

Yes, Bobby ___ right. It ___ n't any of my business. Bobby ___ n't my son. I ___ just an old lady.

Where ___ Mrs. Curtis? What time ___ it?

It ___ 5:30. She ___ usually home at 5:15. Where ___ she? Why ___ she late?

Pronoun Practice

Read the following story. Circle the correct *pronoun*. Do *not* look at the original story.

That's Bobby. Angry? No, ((I) *my me*) am not angry. Bobby is a problem. (*I My Me*) am sorry for (*he his him*). And (*he his him*) mother, (*I my me*) am sorry for (*she her*), too. (*She Her*) is at work all day. Bobby is usually in school, but today (*he his him*) is with those boys. Who are those boys? (*They Their Them*) are new in this neighborhood. Where are (*they their them*) from? (*I My Me*) am worried.

Yes, (*you your*) are right. (*It Its*) isn't any of (*I my me*) business. Bobby isn't (*I my me*) son. (*I My Me*) am just an old lady.

Where's Mrs. Curtis? What time is (*it its?*) (*It It's*) 5:30. (*She Her*) is usually home at 5:15. Where is (*she her*)? Why (*is am are*) she late?

CHAPTER 4

Prepositions

Look at the map in the opposite column. Then, using the map, fill in the empty spaces below.

Examples:

1. The dry cleaners is on Third Avenue across the street from a *restaurant*.
2. The secondhand store is next to a *warehouse*.
3. We are on 88th Street between *our Third Avenue* *second*.

1. The secondhand store is between a _____ and a _____.

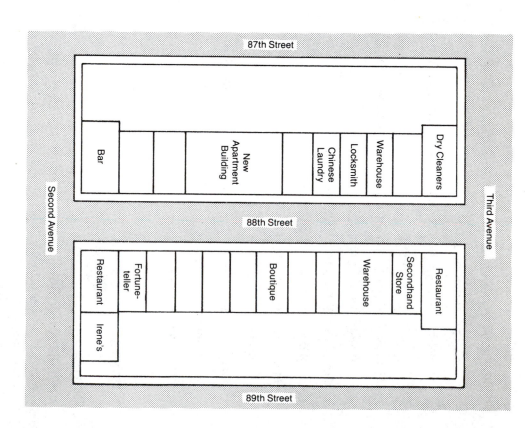

2. The boutique is across the street from the _____.

3. The fortuneteller is next to a _____.

4. The Chinese laundry is between the _____

   and a _____.

5. The locksmith is next to the _____.

Fill in the empty spaces using one of the following prepositions:

   between   √next to   across the street from

Look at the map to decide which preposition to use.

Example:

   The locksmith is _next to_ the Chinese laundry.

1. The restaurant on Second Avenue is _____ "Irene's."

2. The boutique is _____ the new apartment building.

3. The Chinese laundry is _____ the locksmith and a warehouse.

4. The restaurant on Third Avenue is _____ the dry cleaners.

5. The secondhand store is _____ a restaurant and a warehouse.

6. The fortuneteller is _____ a restaurant.

CHAPTER 5

Negative Questions

Look at the following example:

The facts: Bobby is 14.
Friend: Bobby is 15.
   You: Isn't he 14? ← (Notice the *negative* question.)
Friend: Oh, maybe you're right.

Look at the dialogue above. Now fill in the dialogues below with negative questions that have the correct information in them.

1. The facts: Mr. Torres is from Cuba.
   Friend: Mr. Torres is from Columbia.
   You: _____ ?
   Friend: Oh, maybe you're right.

2. The facts: Life is difficult for many people in the U.S.
   Friend: Life is easy for everybody in the U.S.
   You: _____ ?
   Friend: Oh, maybe you're right.

3. The facts: Your friend is home early today.
   Friend: Hello. What time is it?
   You: It's 4:00. _____ ?
   Friend: Yes. I'm usually home at 5:00.

Additional information is frequently given in a negative question. Example:

The facts: San Francisco is in California.

Friend: San Francisco is a very large city.

You: Isn't San Francisco in California?

Friend: Yes. You're right.

Now fill in the dialogues below with negative questions.

1. The facts: Pietro Canepa and his friend are moving to 88th Street.

   Friend: Pietro and Bill are moving.

   You: _____ ?

   Friend: Yes. You're right.

2. The facts: Ms. Cappa is from New York.

   Friend: My teacher's name is Ms. Cappa.

   You: _____ ?

   Friend: Yes. You're right.

3. The facts: Mrs. Curtis is working.

   Friend: Where's Mrs. Curtis?

   You: _____ ?

   Friend: Oh, that's right.

4. The facts: Easter is in April.

   Friend: When's Easter this year?

   You: _____ ?

   Friend: Oh, . . . maybe. But sometimes it's in March.

More Advanced Exercises

Read the following example:

The facts: You're friend's appointment with the dentist is this afternoon.

Friend: I'm going home.

You: (go) Aren't you going to your appointment with the dentist?

Friend: Oh, thanks for reminding me.

Now fill in the dialogues below with negative questions.

1. The facts: Your friend's appointment with the teacher is tomorrow.

   Friend: I'm going to the movies tomorrow.

   You: (go) _____ ?

   Friend: That's right. Thanks for reminding me.

2. The facts: Maria is visiting her cousin in Philadelphia next weekend.

   You: Who are you calling?

   Friend: Maria.

   You: What for?

   Friend: A date.

   You: When?

   Friend: Next weekend.

   You: _____ ?

   Friend: Darn it. That's right. Thanks for telling me.

3. The facts: Yasumi Cho is studying philosophy.

   Friend: Yasumi is interesting.

   You: Who's he?

Friend: She!
You: Who's she?
Friend: She's a friend from Japan.
You: Oh, yes. _____?
Friend: Yes. That's right. She's really intelligent.

CHAPTER 8

Practice in Reading Italics

A word is italicized for emphasis. It is an imitation of the loudness in a person's voice in speaking. Repeat the following sentence or questions after your teacher:

1. Where's your father from?
   Where *is* your father from?
2. You're not alone.
   You're *not* alone.
3. When are you coming home?
   When *are* you coming home?

Note: When you are writing, draw a line under the word(s) you want to emphasize.

I'm listening to you.

I am <u>listening</u> to you.

Read the following conversations with another student. Be sure to emphasize the italicized words.

1. My father's from New York. Where's *your* father from?
   San Juan.
2. Your father's from Mexico, right?
   No.
   No? Where *is* your father from?
   Colombia.
   No kidding.
3. I'm afraid of this street at night.
   Don't worry. You're not alone.
   Who are you talking to?
   I'm alone.
   You're *not* alone. You're talking to someone.
4. Listen. This is important.
   I'm listening.
   Meet me tonight at 9:00 at 3rd Avenue and 88th Street.
   Okay.
   Listen. This is important.
   Yes?
   You're not listening.
   I *am* listening. Go ahead.
   Maria and Franklin are . . .
5. Help, Mom? This is Jacques.
   When are you coming home?
   In half an hour.
   All right. Dinner's almost ready.
   Hello, Mom? I'm not coming home for dinner.
   When *are* you coming home?
   I'm not sure.

CHAPTER 10

Verb Practice

Read the following example:

It's 8:00 A.M. (*Go to school*)

I'm not going to school yet.

Make negative sentences with *yet*.

1. It's May. (*Wear summer clothes*)

_____

2. The sky is cloudy. (*Rain*)

_____

3. It's only 9:00 P.M. (*Go to bed*)

_____

4. It's October. (*Send Christmas cards*)

_____

5. I have $10. (*Go to the bank*)

_____

CHAPTER 11

Comparatives

Read the following examples.

Bob is 21. Sue is 35. Bob is younger than Sue. Sue is older than Bob. James is 73. James is the oldest. Bob is the youngest.

Comparison of two:

younger than
older than

Comparison of one to two or more:

the youngest
the oldest

Make comparisons using *old* and *young*.

1. Compare Bob to James.

Bob is younger than James.

2. Compare Bob to Sue.

_____

3. Compare James to Sue.

_____

4. Compare Sue to Bob.

_____

5. Compare James to Bob.

_____

Juanito is 7 months old. Karl is 2. Billy is 5.
Make comparisons using *young* and *old*.

1. Compare Karl to Juanito.

2. Compare Billy to Juanito.

3. Compare Karl to Billy.

4. Compare Juanito to Billy.

5. Compare Billy to Juanito and Karl.

6. Compare Juanito to Karl and Billy.

Here's a description of Jean's family:

There are five children in my family. The oldest is Mary. Then there's Joan. She's one year younger than Mary. The next one is my brother John. He's two years younger than Joan. Then there's George. He's two years younger than John. I'm the youngest. I'm five years younger than George.

Now tell me about yours:

Look at this.
Compare the buildings using *tall* and *small*.

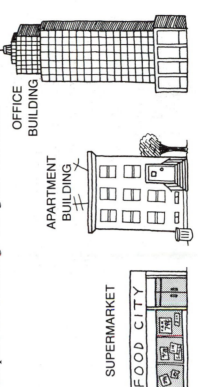

SUPERMARKET

APARTMENT BUILDING

OFFICE BUILDING

FOOD CITY

1. Compare the supermarket and the office building.

2. Compare the apartment building and the super-market.

3. Compare the supermarket and the apartment building.

4. Compare the office building to the apartment building and the supermarket.

5. Compare the supermarket to the other two.

Try this exercise:

1. Compare your apartment building or your house to your classroom building. Use *tall* or *small*.

2. Now compare your home in your country to your home in the U.S. Use *large* or *small*.

Do these two things. Don't write.

1. Ask two friends "How many rooms are there in your apartment or house?"

2. Now, think of how many rooms there are in *your* apartment or house.

Now, write a comparison of your apartment to the others using *large* and *small*.

Do this. Ask two students, "How much is your rent?" Then compare yours to theirs using *high* and *low*. Now do some more. Think of some other things you can ask the other people in your class. Then compare their answer to your answer.

CHAPTER 12

Language Function Practice

Read the following introduction:

John: Mr. Fein, this is my wife, Barbara. Barbara, this is Mr. Fein.

Barbara: Pleased to meet you.

Mr. Fein: How do you do?

Now read this one:

John: Mr. Fein, this is my wife, Barbara. Barbara, Mr. Fein.

Barbara: Hello.

Mr. Fein: It's nice to meet you.

And this one:

John: Mr. Fein, this is Barbara, my wife.

Barbara: How do you do, Mr. Fein?

Mr. Fein: How do you do?

Now write some introductions, or practice them in class with other students.

1. Introduce a friend to your mother or a relative.

_____

2. Introduce your teacher to a friend.

_____

3. Introduce a friend to a neighbor.

_____

CHAPTER 14

Comparatives

Look at the map of Europe on page 190. Then answer the questions below. Use *larger than* or *smaller than* when you answer.

1. Spain is *larger than* Portugal.

2. Italy is _____ Sweden.

3. Belgium is _____ Romania.

4. Hungary is _____ France.

5. Finland is _____ Bulgaria.

6. The Netherlands is _____ Poland.

7. Albania is _____ Yugoslavia.

8. Austria is _____ Germany.

9. Norway is _____ Ireland.

Compare some other countries on the map.

1. _____

2. _____

3. _____

4. _____

5. _____

Look at the map of South America on page 191. Then answer the questions below by writing *the largest* or *the smallest* in the correct spaces.

1. Of the three countries, Brazil, Columbia, and Ecuador, Brazil is *the largest*.

2. Of the three countries, Guyana, Surinam, and Bolivia, Surinam is _____.

3. Of the three countries, Venezuela, Peru, and Paraguay, Peru is _____.

4. Of the four countries, Chile, Argentina, Ecuador, and Uruguay, Argentina is _____.

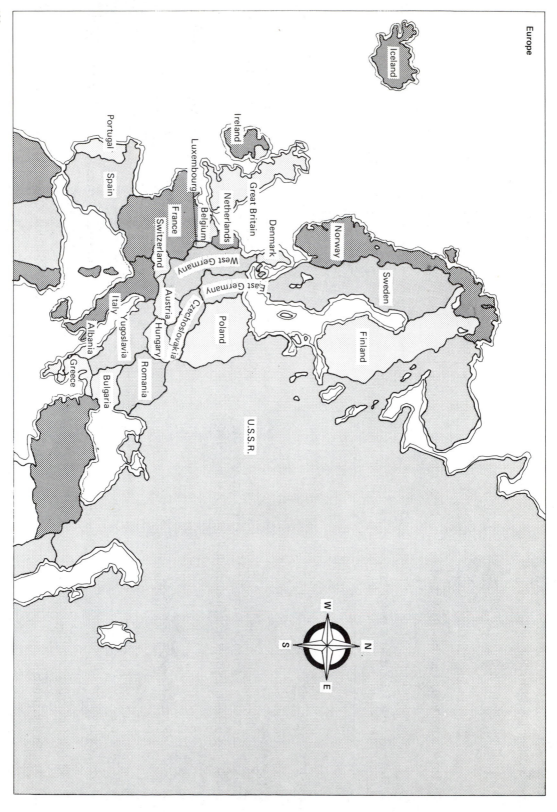

South America

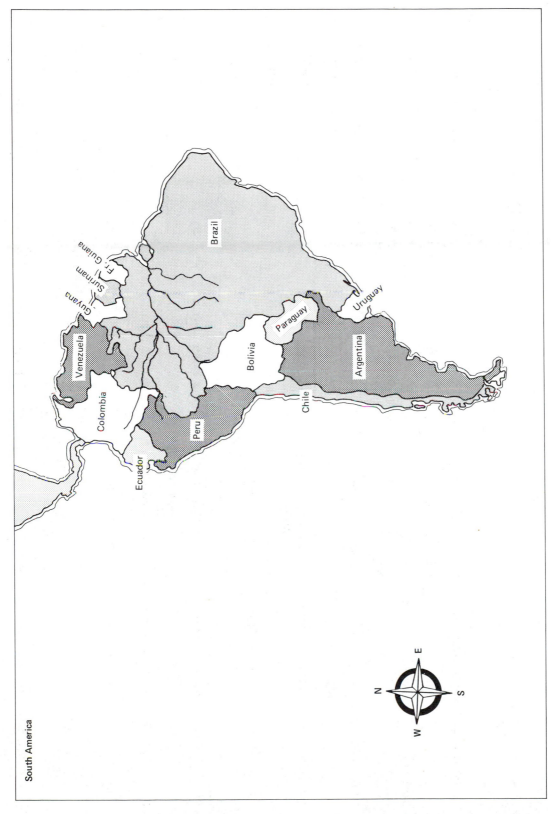

5. Of the four countries, Uruguay, Surinam, French Guiana, and Chile, Chile is _____.

Compare some other countries on the map.

1. _____

2. _____

3. _____

4. _____

5. _____

CHAPTER 15

Verb Practice

Read the following explanation.

After a preposition, use the *-ING Form* of the verb. (A preposition is a word like "in" or "on" or "of.")

I'm tired *of sitting.*
He's interested *in looking* at TV.

After the verb *stop*, use the *-ING Form* of the verb.

Stop *worrying.*
He's going to stop *working* at 5:00.

Basic Form of the Verb	-ING Form of the Verb
sit	sitting
look	looking
work	working
go	going

Do the next exercise. Write the correct form of the verb.

1. I'm not going to sit anymore. I'm tired of *sitting*.

2. I'm not going to go to the laundromat anymore. I'm tired of _____ there.

3. I'm not going to work anymore. I'm tired of _____.

4. I'm not going to cook anymore. I'm tired of _____.

5. I'm not going to eat hamburgers anymore. I'm tired of _____ them.

6. I'm not going to write letters anymore. I'm tired of _____ them.

7. I'm not going to study anymore tonight. I'm tired of _____.

Do this exercise by filling in the correct form of the verb.

1. (learn English)

   He's a good student, so he's interested in _learning English_.

2. (buy a coat)

   Winter is coming, so I'm interested in _____

3. (eat lunch)

   I'm hungry, so right now I'm interested in _____

4. (go to museums)

   He's studying art, so he's interested in _____

5. (read about children)

   She's going to have her first baby, so she's interested in _____

6. (learn the law for tenants)

   They're having trouble with their landlord, so they're interested in _____

7. (buy some furniture)

   He's going to rent his first apartment, so he's interested in _____

8. Write about something you're interested in doing.

   _____
   _____

Do this next exercise by filling in the correct form of the verb.

1. (walk)

   I'm tired. Let's stop _walking_.

2. (talk)

   It's late. Let's stop _____ and go to bed.

3. (study)

   There's a good movie on TV. Let's stop _____ and watch it.

4. (spend so much money)

   We have only $50 in our bank account, so let's stop _____.

5. (*speak Spanish*)
We're always speaking Spanish after class, so let's stop ———— and speak more English.

6. (*buy so much ice cream*)
I'm getting fat, so I'm going to stop ————.

7. (*do this exercise*)
I'm tired now, so I'm going to stop ————.

CHAPTER 17

Verb Practice for More Advanced Students

Gerunds: Use the *-ING Form* of the verb after prepositions.
Look at these examples:

An artist is good at *painting*.
A chef is good at *cooking*.

Now do this exercise.

1. She's an English teacher. (*explain grammar*)
   She's good at explaining grammar.

2. He's a mechanic. (*fix cars*)

3. She's a good student. (*take tests*)

4. He's an interpreter. (*translate*)

5. He's a politician. (*speak in public*)

6. She's a good mother. (*take care of her children*)

7. He's an athlete. (*run fast*)

Can you cook? Can you swim? Can you do math well?
Can you dance? Answer the next question:

What are you good at *doing*?

Look at these examples:

He's afraid of *flying*.
She's afraid of *going* out at night.

Do this exercise.

1. The park can be dangerous at night. (*walk*)
   I'm afraid of walking there at night.

2. Knives can be dangerous. (*cut my hand*)

3. Electricity can be dangerous. (*fix the TV*)

4. Gas can be dangerous. (*light the stove*)

5. Elevators can be dangerous. (*take the elevator*)

6. Cars can be dangerous. (*drive fast*)

7. Snakes can be dangerous. (*hold a snake*)

What animals are dangerous? What sports are dangerous? What other things are dangerous? Answer the next question. Give several answers.

What are many people afraid of doing?

CHAPTER 18

Verb Practice

| am is are | + | verb + *ing* | → Now |

| am is are | + | Going To | + | Verb | → Future |

| Verb | → General |

Look at this:

I'm *reading* now. I usually *get up* at 7:00.
I'm *going to go* to school tomorrow.

A copy of Helen's schedule is on the following page. Take a look at it. Now read this.

Helen: I usually get up at 7:00 on weekdays. After that I eat breakfast. On Saturday and Sunday I get up at 8:00. Monday through Friday I take the bus to work at 8:00. After that I work from 9:00 to 12:00. On Saturday I usually go shopping. On Sunday I go to church. I always eat lunch at 12:00. On Saturday afternoon I do the laundry and clean the apartment. On Sunday I usually walk in the park. I always cook and I eat dinner after 6:00. Weekdays from 7:30 to 11:00 I watch TV or write letters. On Saturday I go to a movie. I usually iron my clothes on Sunday. I always go to bed at 11:00.

Notice the prepositions:

at 7:00	in the morning
at 8:30	in the afternoon
at 9:00	at night
from 9:00 to 12:00	on weekdays
from 1:00 to 5:00	

Now make a schedule for yourself. Make sure you write the time correctly. For example:

= 8:00 (Notice we use *two* periods. It's called a *colon*.)

$1.30 (For money, we use *one* period. It's called a decimal point.)

In your schedule, write the time you get up, the time you leave your apartment, the time you come home, and so forth. Write your schedule on another piece of paper.

Time	Monday	Tuesday	Wednesday	Thursday	Friday	Saturday	Sunday
7:00-	get up - eat				→	get up - eat	get up - eat
8:00-	take the bus to work						
9:00-	work					go shopping	go to church
12:00-	eat lunch						
1:00-	work				→	Do laundry + clean	
5:00-	Return home				→	the apartment	
6:00-	eat dinner				→		
7:00-							
7:30-	watch TV					go to a movie	iron clothes →
11:00-						iron clothes	
11:00	Go to bed				→		

Now answer the following questions. (Use the correct prepositions in your answers.)

1. When do you usually get up on weekdays?
2. When do you leave home?
3. When do you eat lunch?
4. Do you work? When?
5. Do you go to school? When?
6. When do you eat dinner?
7. When do you return home each day?
8. When do you ever watch TV? When?
9. When do you go to bed?

196

	Monday	Tuesday	Wednesday	Thursday	Friday	Saturday	Sunday
12:00							

CHAPTER 19

Rounding Off

$ .50 ⎫
$1.49 ⎭ about $1.00

$1.50 ⎫
$2.49 ⎭ about $2.00

$.50 through $1.49 is rounded off to $1.00; $1.50 through $2.49 is rounded off to $2.00. Look at these examples:

The book is $3.95. *That's about $4.00.*
The record is $5.10. *That's about $5.00.*

Follow the examples, and do this exercise:

1. The shirt is $16.95.
2. The dictionary is $3.95.
3. The rent is $867.55.
4. The clock is $22.79.
5. The sandwich is $3.69.

Practical Mathematics
Look at this example:

a. The bag is reduced from $17.00.
b. It's on sale for $10.95. $17.00
c. That's a saving of $6.05. −$10.95
 $ 6.05

Here's another example:

a. The soup is reduced from $1.05
b. It's on sale for 65¢.
c. That's a saving of 40¢.

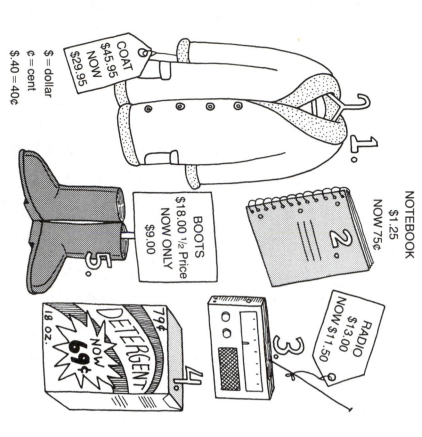

```
   $1.05
 −  .65
   $ .40
```

Soup

Now do the next problems. Write a. *what it is reduced from,* b. *what it is on sale for, and* c. *what the saving is.*

1.

COAT
$45.95
NOW
$29.95

2.

NOTEBOOK
$1.25
NOW 75¢

3.

RADIO
$13.00
NOW $11.50

4.

DETERGENT
79¢
NOW
69¢
18 oz.

5.

BOOTS
$18.00 ½ Price
NOW ONLY
$9.00

$ = dollar
¢ = cent
$.40 = 40¢

Preposition Practice

Look at John's daily schedule:

7:00	get up, wash, etc.
7:30	drink coffee, eat 2 eggs
8:30	leave the apartment
9:00	arrive at work
12:00	go out to lunch
1:00	return to the office
5:00	leave the office
5:30	return home
6:00	eat dinner
7:00	watch television
11:00	watch the news on TV
11:30	go to bed

Now read this paragraph about the schedule. Notice the *prepositions of time.*

He gets up at 7:00. He washes and gets dressed. He eats two eggs and drinks a cup of coffee in the morning. He leaves his apartment at 8:30, and he arrives at work at 9:00. He works from 9:00 to 12:00. At 12:00 he goes out to lunch. He returns and works from 1:00 to 5:00 in the afternoon. At 5:00 he leaves work and returns home. He and Barbara watch TV at night. And finally at 11:30 they go to bed.

Notice: When you use *he* the verb changes. It's necessary to change the Basic Form to the *-S Form.*

Basic Form of the Verb	**-S Form of the Verb**
get up	gets up
eat	eats up
drink	drinks
arrive	arrives
watch	watches
go	goes

Also change the verb to the *-S Form* when you use *she* and *it.*

Now look at Barbara's *weekly* schedule:

Time	Sunday	Monday	Tuesday	Wednesday	Thursday	Friday	Saturday
9:00–12:00	church	work				→	clean apt. buy groceries
12:00–5:00	visit family	work				→	go shopping
6:00	cook dinner and wash dishes						
7:00–11:00		wash clothes	iron clothes	yoga class		yoga class	go out!

Now, on another piece of paper, write a paragraph about Barbara's week. Be sure to use the correct prepositions (Chapter 18), and be sure to use the *-S Form* of the verb when you are writing about Barbara. When you are writing about John *and* Barbara together, use the Basic Form.

1. Divide your class into groups of two or three. Ask each other questions about your daily activities.

When do you leave home?
Do you work?
From when to when?
When do you visit friends or relatives?
What time do you go to bed?

Here are some other possibilities:

eat lunch   return home
go to school   watch TV
eat dinner   go dancing

2. Then tell the rest of the class or write a paragraph using the information you have about one of your class-mates. If you write the paragraph, give it to your class-mate after the teacher returns it to you.

Read the following sentences. Fill in the blanks with the correct prepositions (look in the story on page 115 for the answers you don't know).

1. There's a nice dress ———— the window.

2. You can't live ———— food and water.

3. She's looking at a coat ———— sale.

4. What store is that package ———— ?

5. That color is perfect ———— her.

6. Isn't Carlos too young ———— marriage?

7. The car is reduced ———— $2,000 ———— $1,500.

8. Two ———— his sisters are married.

9. Be careful, ———— heaven's sake!

10. She looks sick. What's wrong ———— her?

11. The refrigerator is full ———— food.

12. What's ———— the package?

Answer the following questions. (Use the correct prepositions.)

1. What's your family doing? (Example: *One of my broth-ers is working in a factory*.)

———————————————————

2. What color is good for you?

———————————————————

3. What do you buy on sale?

———————————————————

4. What's wrong with the shoes you're wearing now?

———————————————————

5. What can't you live without? (in addition to food and water)

———————————————————

CHAPTER 20

Verb Practice

Look at the following:

I was	We were

You were

He was	They were
She was	
It was	

Read the following:

I was in Africa in 1965.

Barbara and John were happy with their new apartment.

Mr. Torres was 52 years old when he came to the U.S.

Assignment

Do you have any pictures of your family? Bring your pictures to class. Tell the class one or two things about your family. Use *was* or *were*. Look at the following examples.

George & His Son John

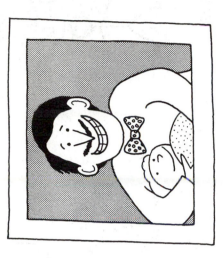

This is George and his baby. George was a fat baby. He was an excellent football player in high school. In the picture, he and his son, John, were at my family's house in Massachusetts.

This is John. He was a very intelligent child. He was also very good at sports like tennis.

This is Peggy. She married Michael in 1978. Before she got married she was a student.

If you don't have any pictures, then make a picture on the blackboard. Like this:

John
(My father)

Emily
(My mother)

CHAPTER 22

Verb Practice

Read the following explanations.

1. *My brother looks like my father.*
   (This means that my father and my brother are similar in appearance.)

2. *That sculpture looks like a horse.*
   (Physically, it is similar to a horse.)

Grammar: look(s) + like + noun or pronoun
          look(s) + like + noun or pronoun + verb
          look(s) + adjective

Fill in the correct form in the following sentences. Use either *looks like* or *looks*.

1. Mary _looks like_ her mother.

2. Helen ———— so happy.

3. Bobby sometimes ———— he has no friends.

4. That tall guy over there ———— a basketball player.

5. Do you think that this sweater ———— good on me?

6. This exercise ———— it's easy.

7. He ———— an average guy, but he's worth 2 million dollars.

Finish the following sentences any way that you wish—but use *looks like* or *looks* in your answer.

1. She's only 23 years old, but she ————————.

2. I look like my mother, but my brother ————————.

3. I know that he's honest, but he ————————.

4. The sky is blue, but it ————————.

5. Her hair is brown, but sometimes in the sun it ————————.

Make some sentences of your own. Describe some people that you know. Describe a place you once visited. Describe some emotions—how do you know when a person is happy, when he is angry, when he is disappointed, when he is excited, etc. Describe how English sounds—use *sounds like* instead of *looks like*. Describe anything you want.